YES *you Can!*

Reaching Your Potential
While Achieving Greatness

Published in the United States by
Insight Publishing Company
707 West Main Street, Suite 5
Sevierville, TN 37862
800-987-7771
www.insightpublishing.com

Editor: Sandra Pinkoski
Cover Design: Emmy Shubert
Interior Format and Design: Dean Lewis

Disclaimer: This book is a compilation of ideas from numerous experts who have each contributed a chapter. As such, the views expressed in each chapter are of those who were interviewed and not necessarily of the interviewer or Insight Publishing.

ISBN-978-1-60013-557-6
10 9 8 7 6 5 4 3 2 1

MESSAGE FROM THE PUBLISHER FOR
YES YOU CAN!

The interviews found in this book are conducted by David Wright, President of ISN Works and Insight Publishing

If you need that extra boost to get where you're going, I can tell you with confidence that this book will provide the advice you need to know that "yes, you can" get there! We are proud to present authors whose chapters will give you some tools to help you along your journey to wherever you want to go.

I have to admit that there have been times in my life when I definitely thought, "No, I can't!" All successful people get discouraged sometimes. But they don't let discouragement stop them. When you've hit a wall, you have to push through, knowing that eventually yes, you can make it.

The authors I interviewed for this book gave me fascinating and innovative ideas about how to push through to achieve that "Yes You Can" mindset. "Yes you can" is a mantra that you can use every day for encouragement. Like the "Little Engine that could" in the children's book, you can say, "Yes I can, yes I can," all the way up the hills in your life until you grasp what you are reaching for.

The preparation for this book was done by way of the authors' education and their impressive experiences in business. But the primary source of their preparation was life itself. Each author's life experiences provided unique insights into what "yes you can" truly means. Their suggestions will help you succeed in every area of life—business and personal.

David E. Wright, President
ISN Works
& Insight Publishing

TABLE OF CONTENTS

CHAPTER 1

Pumping Mental Iron

by Julia Marrocco

David Wright (Wright)

Today we're talking with Julia Marrocco, President of Mental Iron Coaching. She brings more than three decades of business ownership, management, sales, and consulting experience to the marketplace. She's been called the "no-nonsense coach," as well as the "five-foot-tall female Vince Lombardi in high heels." She coaches senior executives and business leaders to leverage their strengths, increase their emotional intelligence, become more disciplined, and build their mental toughness to increase both productivity and bottom line results. Julia is a member of the Institute of Management Consultants and International Coach Federation. She is a Certified Professional Behavior Analyst, an EQ (Emotional Intelligence) Mentor, and an entertaining speaker with a performing arts background.

Julia, welcome to *Yes You Can!*

Julia Marrocco (Marrocco)

Thank you so much; it's a pleasure to be here.

Wright

I know you are currently writing a book about growing up in a ballet studio. What did you learn growing up that you have brought into the business world to help people become better leaders?

Marrocco

Ballet studios are places of discipline and places of constant and consistent practice of the basics. A professional dancer has to be in class or rehearsal on time. Discipline is the foundation, and the dancer practices the basic movements so much they become internalized. The dancer can visually run through them in his or her mind without the music. Internalization makes a performer good. Having said that, there's a difference between good and great. What's missing today in business, the piece the ballet studio brings, is feeling—the emotion. When you add that piece to something already good, you make real magic.

For example, you're the dancer on the stage and you've learned all the steps to your part in Swan Lake. You've rehearsed and rehearsed; you could go out there and do the steps perfectly because you're in shape and you know the steps backward and forward. It would look good. The audience would say you're a competent dancer. But competence isn't enough. You want it to be the performance of a lifetime—something that your audience never forgets. Stepping into the emotion behind the story, behind the music, and behind the choreography will make it the performance of a lifetime.

So what I like to say is, "Discipline and practice create competence. Add passion, and you create magic." For some reason, our business culture is missing its passion and enthusiasm today; yet, it is the very ingredient that makes the magic. It seems we've managed to create a lot of zombies in the corporate world. Disengagement is a huge profit drain on companies, and we know it. We've been talking about it for years, yet the problem is not going away. More employees are on Prozac than ever before. We have leadership issues, which then create culture issues.

I bring in the principles I learned in the studio and on the stage to the corporate world. I "infect" the senior leadership with a "passion virus" that then works its way down the ranks, increasing engagement.

Wright

That makes sense. Talking about Prozac reminds me that you were a rebellious teenage drug-abuser and actually lived on the streets, right? How did that affect what you do in business?

Marrocco

I know, it seems inconsistent with my image now, but it is true. I came from a very good home; it wasn't as if my parents beat me or any of that. I had everything a child could need, and then some, but I just never felt as though I fit in anywhere, including my own family. There was something I was searching for. At thirteen I left home to find it. Of course, what I found was a dangerous, dirty life full of drugs and darkness. The drugs became my friend—a way to escape reality, to make me feel good even in the worst of circumstances.

I'm not proud of that whole time because I lost my innocence and ended up in bondage to my addictions. I personally believe that what God gave me instead was an uncanny gift to be able to "read" people with absolutely no judgment, and to understand people at a level that transcends most human ability in the workplace. Although most of my executive clients aren't addicts, I would be lying if I said there wasn't a lot of addictive behavior and a lot of stress and substance abuse in the workplace. When I do run into dysfunction in the workplace, I'm able to say, "Hey, look, you can't tell me anything that I haven't seen already, so let's work on this." My own personal experience allows me to understand the rough corners of the back stage just as well as the refined appearance of opening night, and all that goes on behind the curtain. If there do happen to be substance abuse issues, I am trained to deal with that in the workplace. Because the element of trust is already there, it is something that we can work with more smoothly and easily.

Wright

You do talk a lot about addiction in the workplace. Would you tell our readers what they should know or be aware of?

Marrocco

I think the main thing is admitting that no matter what your policy in the workplace, abuse and addiction are all around us. What we need to be aware of is this: No one is immune, and addictive behavior crosses all ethnic, socio-economic, and demographic boundaries. Nearly 75 percent of all adult illicit drug users are employed, as are most binge and heavy alcohol users. The number one prescribed drug in the United States is Vicodin, to the tune of 123.3 million prescriptions, and 1.78 billion (that's with a "b") dollars in retail.

Studies show that substance-abusing employees are more likely to change jobs frequently, be late to or absent from work, be less productive, be involved in a workplace accident, file a workers' compensation claim, and so on.

Let's be realistic, we're human. We all have some kind of weakness. Some of us have the kind that comes out more when we're stressed, perhaps in an angry outburst, perhaps we have a tendency to eat when we're anxious, or stay up and play video games all night to "escape." Perhaps it's something a little more harmful. Everyone is different and you can't read genetic code at an interview (at least not yet). We're not all as disciplined as we'd like to be. You never know where and when illness will strike on the job, whether it's cancer, MS, or substance addiction.

Your company leadership needs to be aware, and each leader needs to be a role model. So if there's a problem, attack it swiftly by getting the professional help needed. Suspend judgment—illness is illness, whether it's mental or physical.

Wright

What are the watershed moments that ended up making you one of the thought leaders in executive performance?

Marrocco

Interestingly, they are all moments when a mentor said something that resonated. We probably all have at least one memory of something that a parent, teacher, or other role model said at some point that went *"Ping!"* and stuck with us forever.

My first watershed moment in business was the afternoon in Vancouver, Washington, when I went to see Jim Rohn for the first time. He said (my paraphrase), "Work hard at your job and you'll make yourself a living; work hard on yourself and you'll make yourself a fortune." It was as if he had hit me in the head with a hammer! My late husband and I owned a Real Estate company and were partners in a farm machinery business at the time. Both were fairly new businesses for my husband and me. I was already working as hard, as fast, and as much as I could, and there weren't any more days in a week. I couldn't get another hour in the day, and I couldn't spend another hour awake for lack of sleep. Both businesses were providing livings for other families than our own—our money was going back into the business and we never knew how the next mortgage payment was going to be made. I was about at the end of my rope. I had already given up my passion (teaching ballet) to help the business stay afloat, and wasn't having a very fun life. I was full of self-pity and anger at my husband for "putting me in this position."

So when I heard Jim say that, it was as though he had opened a new door for me. I began to think about what I needed to work on. When I started working on my own self-development, I began to enjoy life, bloom where I was planted for the time being, looked for the lessons, practiced becoming more "present," and I doubled my income.

My income doubled again the following year, and in the process, I became a new and improved version of myself. I hired my first executive coach, and simultaneously began coaching others on their performance (rather than managing them). I realized that his advice to me—the discipline of working on yourself—is the secret to everything.

Everyone around us began to be more successful and, by looking in the mirror and asking ourselves the tough questions, we all got better. It all started with Jim just saying that one sentence. It took me back to what I knew to be true from the ballet studio. Look in the mirror, practice those small improvements, and keep working on yourself.

My second watershed moment was a couple of years ago when Charlie ("Tremendous") Jones celebrated his eightieth birthday. I was talking to him on and off toward the end of his life and he said, "Julia, there is one thing you've got to do—you've got to carry the torch after I die, and keep people reading." I promised him I would. I have given away hundreds of copies of *The Fred Factor* by Mark Sanborn, *Think and Grow Rich* by Napoleon Hill, *Life is Tremendous* by Charlie himself, and so on. He was always so passionate about reading. He died not long after that, but I have taken his charge seriously and will never drop the ball on that promise. It is a command I will obey.

Jim Rohn was a great reader of books, too. He always talked about library cards and if they're free, why doesn't everyone own one? Two thirds of Americans have a library card and most don't use it more than a few times a year. In any case, the wisdom of the ages is in books and nothing will propel you faster into the world of success than reading. My clients who read a lot are the best leaders in the corporate world. The information you need to transform yourself, your career, your results, your relationships, and anything else you want, is between the covers of the books on the shelves of your local bookstore or library.

My third watershed moment was during a conference with another mentor, Dr. Lance Wallnau (another great reader of books). During a conference in Mexico, he encouraged me to bring my spirituality to the workplace and it allowed me to be even more bold and effective. (My clients reading this are thinking *more* bold? How is that possible?) With Charlie Jones and Jim Rohn both gone now, Dr. Lance is my remaining mentor, along with my executive coach, R. Alan Smith, and my loving husband, Dante, from whom I get my inspiration every day.

Wright

We've been hearing a lot about emotional intelligence these days, and I know you're a known thought leader in that subject. What part does that play in the businesses you work with?

Marrocco

Well, David, right now, we have what I call an "emotional intelligence shortage crisis" in government and corporate leadership. There is such a lack of empathy! We have a huge problem with disengagement in the workplace, as I mentioned before. It's coming from the top down and I know people want to kill the messenger sometimes, but frankly, we need to work on this area.

There have been a lot of studies since Daniel Goleman came out and gave EQ the attention and credibility it deserved in *The Harvard Business Review*. Dr. Izzy Justice has done a lot of work in the EQ field, as have many others, including Paul Ekman, and my friend, Dr. Ken Hill, from the Institute of Management Consultants, who wrote *Smart Isn't Enough*.

What we have discovered is that CEOs generally test very low on emotional intelligence. That's the bad news. The good news is that emotional intelligence can be learned and improved. Unlike IQ, which can't be improved, you can train and coach to gaps in EQ. I do lots of EQ (also called EI) testing and coaching. Every leader out there should have his or her EQ tested and work with an executive coach to improve it. If every corporate leader had just a little more empathy, our employee loyalty, buy-in, and engagement would improve, along with the company's bottom line.

Wright

Talk about Mental Iron for a moment. Why did you name your company that and what is "Mental Iron" anyway?

Marrocco

A lot of people ask me that. The name came from thinking about how we keep our bodies in shape. We go to the gym and we pump iron—we lift weights. That's an important part of keeping ourselves in shape, right? If we would add a similar amount of time to our schedule to read, ponder, and brainstorm, what could we do for our mind? So, again, it goes back to reading, self-development, learning, asking questions, researching, discussing, debating, discerning, and thinking. That's why I named the practice "Mental Iron." It is the strategists, the thinkers, who make the history that goes into the books and teaches others.

Here's the magic question: What are you reading right now that is changing you for the better? What are you reading that is making you a better spouse, a better parent, a better coach, a better mentor, a better role model, a better CEO? Leaders need to take the time to think on a daily basis. Unfortunately, what's happened is this: both our reading and our thinking have taken a backseat to our "getting stuff done." Yes, personal productivity is important, but someone needs to be thinking about why we're doing what we're doing, and communicating it to the front line.

Wright

You're big on your clients having a personal vision and mission and aligning it with their company's vision and mission. What's your own vision and how does that play out in the day-to-day work that you do?

Marrocco

Having a personal vision is critical, and you'd better hope it aligns in some way with your company's vision (at the very least that it doesn't conflict with it!). The culture of the company is built on how the leader(s) behave. This behavior passes the culture down, and brands the company. Everyone's individual vision doesn't have to necessarily be the same as that of every other person who works in the company, but it has to be in alignment, and it really helps if the person has some passion surrounding the vision, because that creates excitement and momentum. Anyone whose vision conflicts or doesn't buy in is stealing his or her paycheck from the company because he or she is not engaged. Everyone has to have some "skin in the game." Any CEO who is not moved emotionally by the organization's vision should step down. Strong words, I know, but look at our corporate world today and tell me I'm wrong.

Our vision is what calls us to wake up in the morning and calls us to move throughout the day and to keep on going when we're tired and to overcome obstacles that get in our way.

My personal vision is to abolish modern-day slavery. That vision is so large that it cannot be done in my lifetime. My grandchildren's grandchildren will probably still be working to abolish slavery. William Wilberforce worked his entire work life in British Parliament to stop the slave trade in Britain. Here in the United States, Abraham Lincoln proclaimed the emancipation of American slaves. Yet in today's world, slavery is more rampant than ever. In the 1850s the cost of a slave was around forty thousand dollars in today's money. Today, a human being can be purchased for between sixteen and fifty dollars, even in our own country! The vision of true freedom for every person and the sacred dignity of each person on this globe is what carries me through the day. My work with leaders and my conversations on the street with people all point to that and align with it.

Much bondage is self-imposed by our own feelings of victimization, our finances, our addiction to substances, anger, power, or whatever. That's all slavery, too. Sadly much slavery is self-imposed by those of us who have the luxury of freedom.

Wright

What's the biggest struggle that you see your clients go through when you're coaching them?

Marrocco

Well, the biggest struggle with my senior executive clients is to get them to suspend judgment. First, judgment about executive coaching itself—what it is, what it isn't, and the fact that everyone needs a coach. Frequently, the response to coaching is, "I don't need it because I don't have any problems right now." Well, the whole idea of coaching is not about fixing a problem; fixing is for attorneys, doctors, and therapists.

A coach is someone to help accelerate what you are doing and help you be more successful in your job and your life, thereby making both more rewarding. Coaching is both a relationship and a process. Professional athletes, performers, writers, and successful politicians don't say, "As soon as I start having a problem, I'll hire a coach." No! They hire a coach in the beginning because they recognize the importance of someone who can come alongside them and hold the mirror, hold them accountable, and encourage them to keep going when times get tough. It's like the difference between having a personal trainer at the gym and working out on your own. You will never do that extra repetition without the trainer. Smart executives realize that a coach is someone they need to have on board, not just sometimes, but always. Sometimes people think coaching is remediation. For example, the board of directors sends a message to the HR Department saying, call a coach and come in and "fix" this guy. I do get those calls, and rarely will I take the job. When it's remediation time, it's usually too late.

The second struggle my clients go through (once they understand and embrace coaching) is the letting go and being vulnerable to someone. It's a confidential relationship in coaching, but being vulnerable and opening yourself up is hard sometimes. Trusting is hard when you're at the top; it takes time. The more there is at stake, the more careful you become.

Beyond the misunderstanding of what coaching is, and the difficulty of trusting, the third thing clients struggle with is respect—both giving it and getting it. The return of respect in the workplace (not to mention in families and marriages) is another mission of mine. In our global situation, we are missing a huge piece in relationships with each other, and that piece is respect. This is usually due to a lack of understanding and a lack of exposure that puts us out of our comfort zone. Now, more than ever, we need to have behavioral and generational diversity training.

Wright

You've talked about Jim Rohn and Charlie "Tremendous" Jones; who are some of your other heroes and the people who have helped you shape the way you coach others?

Marrocco

Vince Lombardi—the *man*. He was already forty-six years old when he took the head coach job with the Packers, and he turned them around in one year from a losing team to a seven to five record. Then, during the next eight years, they won six divisional and five NFL championships, and two Super Bowls! That's great coaching! He said, "Running a football team is no different than running any other kind of organization—an army, a political party, or a business. The principles are the same." He was all about winning. He was tougher than tough, but he had tremendous love for his players and for the game.

Wright

I used to marvel at the stories about Lombardi. When he lost a game he was back there Monday morning and saying, "Gentleman, this is a football." Now, *that's* going back to basics.

Marrocco

Exactly, right. It's *all* about the basics. He was about all the things we've talked about: discipline, practice, internalization, mental toughness, emotional intelligence, and passion.

Wright

So what do you think are the most important qualities a person must possess to be a great leader?

Marrocco

Vision, passion, ability to be strategic, emotional intelligence, humility, and authenticity.

Wright

What do you think of executives who are doing really well already— why do they need a performance coach?

Marrocco

There are a number of reasons. First of all, they need to continue growing. We have a new band of "young guns" to be reckoned with in the workforce. They are coming on strong, and they do a lot of reading and a lot of learning. They're very smart, they're very active, they can be somewhat rebellious, and they're pushing through. They expect the best out of their leaders and they believe they know more than their leader. We've got to keep up with those guys; they are amazingly bright and independent. So the first reason executives need a performance coach is to stay agile.

Another reason to have a coach is for grooming people for a succession plan. We've got to be looking at our pool of who is going to replace the next guy who's apt to retire or leave. I just read some stats this morning from Dr. Justice, who reported that 54 percent of working Americans state that they are likely to look for new jobs once the economy rebounds. Forty-nine percent of employees say pay raises will be the most effective retention tool right after the recovery; right now they're hanging on to jobs, and 83 percent of employers have to increase their communication to keep their employees engaged.

There are a lot of people who are ready to jump ship; they don't want to lose the job they have, but they're not truly happy there. In order to keep the people we have, and/or get the people we want, we have to be our very, very best. A coach is a valuable asset for succession-planning, for finding the right people, finding our significance in life, even enjoying our own job. There are many CEOs right now who are not very happy. It's tough—can you imagine running a Fortune 500 company right now? You're on the line; your head is on the chopping block. For personal growth, for finding balance, significance in life, for succession planning, mentoring, grooming, and just dealing with the day-to-day stuff that gets thrown at you, you have to bring your "A" game and you cannot bring your "A" game without a coach!

When is the last time you saw any performance on stage without a director, any kind of music without a conductor, any kind of sport without a coach? It just doesn't happen, and yet we allow it to happen in the corporate world; what in the world are we thinking?

Wright

What do you think are the biggest mistakes you see leaders make in the business world today?

Marrocco

I've got to be honest; there was something that was hitting me today as I was writing. I was thinking about complacency and how tired we are as a corporate culture. America seems tired. We've gone through this "traumatic" economy, and the bullets are flying through board rooms across the country. For the last twenty-four months or so, many people have been fighting off dragons.

Recently, someone coined the term "a no-motion" (as opposed to a promotion). This term refers to when an employee gets more responsibility with no increase in pay and no new title. I witness a lot of people working overtime and being out of "work-life" balance, doing what used to be three people's jobs, and not having the support staff they used to have. This will work on a temporary basis, but it's not sustainable. Some people are just worn out. They are re-evaluating why they are doing this— is it worth it, and why? Into their life sneaks complacency. And complacency is one of those sneaky "viruses" that says, "Oh, I'm good enough—I don't need to take that extra step. I don't need to do that extra pushup. I don't need to listen to Coach Lombardi and show up at practice on time. I'm tired; no one will notice if I go in at nine o'clock instead of eight-thirty." Complacency is like a cancer, it slowly kills us from the inside out. You don't see it at first, and then all of a sudden you can't figure out why things are falling apart. If the leader is tired, the troops' lives are in danger.

That's what I notice today. Tomorrow I might say something else, but today that's really been on my heart. Complacency is the biggest mistake that leaders can make. They need to be on the edge every day, flying the vision flag, because the vision is so important that it's what will keep everyone you lead going, too. A flag leads men and women into battle, yes? No flag, no courage, no work. And the enemy wins. The most passionate, excited team wins. The question is, will it be you or your opponent?

Wright

Well, what a great conversation. I really appreciate all this time you've taken to answer these questions. You've given me a lot to think about here. We have a lot of friends and mentors in common.

Marrocco

Oh, it's been so much fun, David! I appreciate your time, too. God bless you.

Wright

Today we've been talking with Julia Marrocco. Julia coaches senior executives and business and community leaders to leverage their brainpower, increase their emotional intelligence, be more disciplined, and build their mental toughness to increase their productivity and the resulting bottom line results.

Julia, thank you so much for being with us on *Yes You Can!*

Marrocco

Thank you David, and you have a blessed day.

Julia Marrocco is an executive coach and business consultant who works with senior executives and community leaders to improve their performance, presence, and power.

She uses a full range of scientifically validated assessments for talent management, leadership development, job benchmarking, and performance metrics. She spends half her time in the corporate world working with high-powered executives and half her time on the streets and in homeless shelters where she does drug and alcohol counseling, reconciliation coaching, and life skills training. She is a social activist against sex trafficking and other forms of modern-day slavery, as well as a spokesperson for disabled, at-risk, and marginalized populations, and speaks on the stigma of mental illness. She also speaks to community leaders about the benefits of mentorship through organizations such as Big Brothers Big Sisters.

Julia is passionate about the subject of the brain. She is a Certified Professional Behavior Analyst and a member of the NeuroLeadership Institute. She is a popular speaker on the West Coast circuit for her high-octane "Pumping Mental Iron" keynotes and workshops.

Marrocco grew up in Ithaca, New York. She now lives with her husband in Portland, Oregon, and has a second home in La Jolla, California. In her "self" time you will find her at a ballet performance, the symphony, the theater, the library, or a museum. She studies Pilates and Yoga, and loves to hike.

Julia Marrocco
PO Box 5246
Portland, Oregon 97208
503-750-3950
julia@mentaliron.com
www.mentaliron.com

CHAPTER 2

Becoming A Leader

by Warren Bennis

David Wright (Wright)

Today we are talking with Warren Bennis, PhD. He is a university professor and a distinguished professor of business at the University of Southern California and chairman of USC's leadership institute. He has written eighteen books, including *On Becoming a Leader, Why Leaders Can't Lead,* and *The Unreality Industry,* coauthored with Ivan Mentoff. Dr. Bennis was successor to Douglas McGregor as chairman of the organizational studies department at MIT. He also taught at Harvard and Boston universities. Later he was provost and executive vice president of the State University of New York atBuffalo and president of the University of Cincinnati. He published over nine hundred articles. Two of his books have earned the coveted McKenzie Award for the "Best Book on Management." He has served in an advisory capacity for the past four U.S. presidents, and consultant to many corporations and agencies and to the United Nations. Awarded eleven honorary degrees, Dr. Bennis has also received numerous awards including the Distinguished Service Award from the American Board of Professional Psychologists and the Perry L. Ruther Practice Award from the American Psychological Association.

Dr. Bennis, welcome to *Yes You Can!*

Warren Bennis (Bennis)

I'm glad to be here again with you, David.

Wright

In a conversation with *Behavior Online*, you stated that most organizations devaluate potential or emerging leaders by seven criteria: business literacy, people skills, conceptual abilities, track record, taste, judgment, and character. Because these terms were somewhat vague, you left them to be defined by the reader. Can we give our readers an unadorned definition of these criteria, as you define them?

Bennis

There's no precise dictionary definition that would satisfy me or maybe anyone. I'll just review them very quickly because there's a lot more we want to discuss.

Business literacy really means: do you know the territory, do you know the ecology of the business, do you know how it works, do you know where the plugs are, do you know who the main stakeholders are, and are you familiar with a thing called business culture?

People skills: This is your capacity to connect and engage, because business leadership is about establishing, managing, creating, and engaging in relationships. Conceptual abilities is more important these days because it has to do with the paradoxes and complexities—the cartography—of stakeholders that make life at the top (more than ever) interesting and difficult, which is why we've had such a turnover in CEOs and leaders over the last few years.

Track record: Now, if I want to know about a person—if I were a therapist—one of the first questions I would ask is, "Tell me about your job history." That tells me a lot. On the whole, as my dad used to say, "People who get A's are smart." People who have a successful track record tend to be effective. We don't always go on that, because sometimes these people don't grow. But, if I had only one measuring stick, it would be that one: Tell me your job history. Let's talk about whether it looks successful or whether you view it as successful or not. It's hard to define, but it's about whether or not you have the capacity a good curator has, a good selector has, to know people. It's always a tough one; God knows we all make mistakes. Your taste means your capacity to judge other people in relation to the other six characteristics.

I think taste and judgment are combined. I dealt with them separately because I thought taste was specifically the selection of people in an intuitive and objective way, but also in a subjective way. It has to do with the range of such things as being bold versus being reckless. It has to do with the strategic implications and consequences of any decision and what you take into account in making any decision, especially the tough ones. The easy ones are different; everyone looks good in a bull market. It's when things get tough, vulnerable, difficult, and in a crisis mode that judgment really counts the most. Taste and judgment are the hardest things to learn, let alone teach.

Character: Here I have in mind a variety of things such as size of ego, the capacity to listen, emotional intelligence, integrity, and authenticity—basically, is this a person I can trust? That's what character is all about.

Wright

You said that businesses get rid of their top leaders because of lapses in judgment and lapses in character, not because of business literacy or conceptual skills. Why do you think this is true?

Bennis

It's true simply because it's true. Look at the record. I wasn't just stating a hypothesis there that looks to be proved. I was stating experiences with leaders and I'll give you three quick examples.

Howell Raines had the top job in journalism in the world. He had great ideas, great business literacy, and all the things in the top five. He did not have taste, judgment, or character. This is a guy who had an ego the size of Texas. He played favorites, had the best ideas, was a terrific newspaperman and no one would argue with that. But, his way of treating people—of not harnessing the human harvest that was there, and his bullying, brutalizing, arrogant behavior and his inability to listen; that's what I mean by character.

Eckhart Pfeiffer was fired after seven or eight very good years at Compaq. He had terrific ideas, but he did not listen to the people. He was only listening to those on his "A" list who were saying, "Aye, aye, sir." People on his "B" list were saying, "You'd better look at what Gateway and Dell are doing; they're eating our lunch on our best china." He didn't listen; he didn't want to listen. That's what I mean by character. Let me just stay with those two examples, I don't think it's ever about conceptual abilities—ever. There may be some examples I just don't know about. But, with over fifty years of leadership research, I don't know of any leader who has lost his or her job or has been ousted because of a lack of brainpower.

Wright

You said that teaching leadership is impossible, but you also said leadership can be learned. How can that be?

Bennis

Let me qualify that. I teach the stuff, so no, it isn't impossible to teach you. As is the case with everything, teaching and learning are two different things. One has to do with input into people; the other has to do with whether or not they get it. You know very well—and your listeners and readers know very well—that there's a difference between listening to a lecture and it having any influence on you. You can listen to a brilliant lecture and nothing may happen. So, there's a disconnect to teaching and learning.

Actually, how people learn about leadership varies a lot. Most people don't learn about leadership by getting a PhD, or by reading a book, or by listening to a tape, although that may be helpful. They learn it through work and experience. You can be helped by terrific teaching from a recording, a tape, a book, or a weekend retreat.

Basically, the way people learn about leadership is by keeping their eyes open, being a first-class "noticer," having good role models, and being able to see how they deal with life's adversities. You don't learn leadership by reading books. They are helpful, don't get me wrong. I write books; I want them to be read. The message you are trying to get out to your people—to listen and to read—is also important. I think it's terrific. That's my life's work. That's what I do for a living, and I love it. I'll tell you, it has to be augmented by the experiences you face in work and in life.

Wright

Trust me, I have learned, after reading many of your books, that they are teaching materials.

Bennis

Thank you. I hope you also learn from them, David.

Wright

As I was reading those books, I wondered why I did the things you said to do, and they worked when I did it. It's simply because I learned by doing.

Bennis

Thank you. I'm really glad to hear that.

Wright

Since leadership is where the big money, prestige, and power is, why would seasoned business executives, who are monitored more closely than the average employee, let character issues bring them down? One would think it would be like a person who constantly uses profanity, just deciding not to curse in church.

Bennis

I wish it were that easy. It's a really good question. I wish I knew the answer, but I don't. I will give you a real quick example. Howell Raines, as I said before, executive editor of the *New York Times* (people would die to get that position) was an experienced newspaperman, and there was a seventeen-thousand-word article about him in *New Yorker*, June 6, 2002 (he had been on the job since September 2001, so it was written not a year later). The article exposed him; it was a very frank and interesting article. It called him arrogant, a bully, playing favorites, all the things I said earlier, and called him a hell of a good man and a terrific editor. He'd been around the track; he had business literacy up the wah-zoo. He was as good as they get.

He read that article and everybody at the *New York Times* read it. Do you think it might have made him want to change a little bit? Did Julius Caesar not hear the warnings, "Beware the Ides of March?" Did he not hear, "Don't go to the forum?" There were so many signals and he wasn't listening. Why wasn't he listening? Didn't he go down to the newsroom and talk to those people? No. The most common and fatal error is that because of arrogance they stopped listening. It could happen internally, as in the case of Howell Raines, or like Eckhart Pfeiffer, who wasn't listening to his "B" list tell him about Gateway and Dell.

I don't have the answer to your question, but I will tell you, someone ought to be around to remind these people of the voices, stakeholders, and audiences they aren't listening to. That's a way of dealing with it—making sure you have a trusted staff that isn't just giving you the good news.

Wright

I've often thought that if I had been Nixon, I would have burned the tapes, apologized, and moved on.

Bennis

Absolutely.

Wright

I think it's the arrogance factor; you really "hit the nail on the head" when you said that, to put it in my simple terms.

How do people experience leadership when they haven't yet become a leader?

Bennis

How do you become a parent for the first time? There's no book that you are going to read on becoming a parent any more than there is a book you are going to read on becoming a leader that will prepare you for that experience. You're going to fall on your face, get up, dust yourself off, and go on. The only things you're going to learn from are your experiences and having someone around you can depend on for straight, reflective back-talk. A lot of it is breaks, and chance. Some of it isn't that, but if there's one thing I want to underscore, nobody is prepared the first time they are going to be in the leadership position. You're going to fall on your face, you're going to learn from it, and you're going to continue that for the rest of your life.

Wright

At one time, I had a company with about 175 people working for me; we had business in the millions. I just kept making so many mistakes that afterward, I did wish I had read some of the things you had written about before I made those mistakes. It sure would have been helpful.

In your studies, you found that failure, not success, had a greater impact on future leaders—leaders learn the most by facing adversity. Do you think teachers at the college level make this clear?

Bennis

I can't speak for all teachers at the college level. Do you mean people teaching leadership and business management at the college level?

Wright

Yes.

Bennis

I don't know if they do. But, I would imagine things are much more difficult and complicated today because of the kinds of things that business leaders are facing. This includes problems such as globalization, fierce Darwinian competitiveness, complexity of the problems, regulatory pressures, changes in demography, difficulty of retaining your best talent, the price of terrific human capital and then keeping them, the ability to help create a climate that encourages collaboration, and then there's the world danger since 9/11.

Wright

In my case, I just remember the equations and things in the courses I took, such as controlling and directing and those kinds of things. I don't remember anybody ever telling me about exit strategies or what's going to happen if my secretary gets pregnant and my greatest salesperson is the one responsible for it. Who do I fire? As the owner of a small company that's growing at a rapid pace, what can I do to facilitate the competencies of the people I have chosen to lead this into the future?

Bennis

Your company is how big, again?

Wright

I was talking before about a Real Estate conglomerate. Presently I have a speakers' bureau/servicing agency and publishing business. I employ about twenty-five people, and we also use about fifty vendors, which I look at as employees.

Bennis

Yes, they are, aren't they? That's a good way of thinking about it. There are several things you can do in any size company, but with a small company, you can get your arms around it—conceptually, anyway. The leader/owner has to model the very behaviors he or she wants others to model. If you are espousing something that is antithetical to your behavior, then that's going to be a double bind. That's number one.

The second thing is to make leadership development an organic part of the activities at the firm. In addition to encouraging people to read, bringing in people to talk to them, and having retreats, every once in a while look at leadership competencies and what people can do to sharpen and enhance those capacities that are needed to create a culture where people can openly talk about these issues. All of those things can be used to create a climate where leadership development is a part of the everyday dialogue.

Wright

If you were helping me choose people to assume leadership roles as my company grows, what characteristics would you suggest I look for?

Bennis

I've implied some of them early on when I mentioned those seven characteristics. I've become a little leery of the whole selection process; there is some evidence that even interviews don't give you really valid insight. I think what I would tend to do is look at the track record. Talk about that with people—where they think they have failed, where they think they have succeeded. Try to get a sense of their capacity to reflect on issues and see to what extent they have been able to learn from their previous experiences.

See what you can make of how realistically they assess a situation. Most people rarely attribute any blame to themselves; they always think, "The dog ate my homework." It's always some other agent outside of themselves who is to blame. Those are the things that I think are going to be characteristics of emerging leaders among men and women. That's what I would look for—the capacity to reflect and learn.

Wright

When you made that comment about interviews, I don't feel as inept as I did before this conversation. The longer I live, I just feel that when people come in and interview, I want to give them an Academy Award as they walk out. People can say almost anything convincingly in this culture. It's very, very difficult for me to get through, so that's one thing I really had not thought of. It seems so simple though—just follow the track record.

Bennis

I have had the same experience you've had. When I was president of the university and making lots of choices all the time, my best was hitting 700, which means I was off three out of ten times. I think my average here was 60/40; it's rough. It's even harder these days because of legal restrictions, how much you can say about their references, how much they can reveal. We have to pay attention to selection level, no kidding. We can overcome mistakes in the selection level by the culture and how it will screen out behaviors that are not acceptable. That's our best default—the culture itself will so educate people that even the mistakes we make will be resurrected by the culture being our best friend and ally.

Wright

As a leader, generating trust is essential. You have written extensively on this subject. Will you give our readers some factors that tend to generate trust?

Bennis

People want a leader who exudes that they know what he or she is doing. They want a doctor who is competent and they want a boss who really knows his or her way around. Secondly, you want someone who is really on your side—a caring leader. Thirdly, you want a leader who has directness, integrity, congruity, who returns calls, and is trustworthy, who will be there when needed and cares about you and about your growth. Those are the main things. It's not just individuals involved.

A boss must create a climate within the group that provides psychological safety—a holding pattern where people feel comfortable in speaking openly. I think that's another key factor in generating and establishing trust.

Wright

It is said that young people these days have less hope than their parents. What can leaders do to instill hope in their employees?

Bennis

All (and you can emphasize *all)* the leaders I have known have a high degree of optimism and a low degree of pessimism. They are, as Confucius said, "purveyors of hope." Look at Reagan; in a way, look at Clinton and Martin Luther King, Jr. These are people who have held out an idea of what we could become and made us proud of ourselves, created noble aspirations—sometimes audacious, but noble. Leaders have to express in an authentic way that there is a future for our nation and that you have a part in developing that future with me.

Wright

Dr. Bennis, thank you for being with us today, and for taking so much time to answer these questions.

Bennis

Thank you for having me.

Warren Bennis has written or edited twenty-seven books, including the best-selling *Leaders* and *On Becoming a Leader*; both of which have been translated into twenty-one languages. He has served on four U.S. presidential advisory boards and has consulted for many Fortune 500 companies, including General Electric, Ford, and Starbucks. The *Wall Street Journal* named him one of the top ten speakers on management in 1993 and 1996, and *Forbes* magazine referred to him as "the dean of leadership gurus."

Warren Bennis
www.WarrenBennis.com

CHAPTER 3
The Sweet Spot:
The Intersection Where Experience, Finance, Execution, and Courage Meet

by Natalie Cole

David Wright (Wright)

Today we are talking to Natalie Cole. Natalie, a thirty-year newspaper veteran, is a known entity in the world of print media having spent twenty-three years in general market, two years in alternative, and five years in ethnic press. She is CEO of *Our Weekly*, the largest audited circulating black-owned newspaper in Southern California. In 2007, she also founded the Urban Media Foundation, an after-school program that features journalism, technology, and entrepreneurialism for youth.

Natalie's intense entrepreneurial spirit comes from decades of experience gained while leading revenue-generating teams for the Tribune Company. She was *The Los Angeles Times* Director of Classified Inside Sales and Recycler Director of Classified.

Natalie, welcome to *Yes You Can!*

Wright

What is your leadership philosophy?

Natalie Cole (Cole)

My leadership philosophy is to lead by example, demonstrating a high level of integrity, and being respectful of people while doing business responsibly with the fundamental goal to drive a healthy profit margin. As a business management major in college, I learned the difference between official and unofficial leadership. Those who are promoted into management have official leadership, and others in the organization are supposed to follow their lead. In comparison, unofficial leadership occurs when people who do not necessarily have an official capacity, function, or title can and do inspire and influence others in the organization to follow their lead and to behave in ways that accomplish the goals of the company. The capacity to lead unofficially is thought to occur because the person is personally liked, well informed, experienced, and/or respected.

Wright

I know that you are in an official leadership capacity, but based on your experience, has your success also been attributed to unofficial leadership results?

Cole

Yes, I gained great results in my official capacity as a leader, but I also believe that my unofficial influence inspired results beyond that which was expected. I believe that the best leaders are a hybrid of the two—they have the official responsibility and unofficially, others will follow them for very different reasons.

Approximately twenty years ago, I interviewed for an outside retail sales middle-level management position at *The Los Angeles Times*. The division was to be a newly formed team comprised mostly of outside account executives. I had a great track record as a supervisor in classified inside sales, but I was competing against at least two seasoned contenders. Some people considered them more experienced than I, because they were working in outside retail sales at the time. My manager attempted to convince me not to interview, and his words were harsh: "You don't have a snowball's chance in hell of getting that position, so just ask for an informational interview to put your name out there for future opportunities."

I, however, have always had a never-ending, *"yes I can"* attitude. Therefore, I went forward with the interview process without consideration of his negative comment, and I made a lasting impression. I got the job.

Directly following my official promotion as their manager, it became apparent to me that the sales team struggled with the idea that I, with my inside classified sales skills set, would be their manager. Most of the sales team did not know my record or me. I later found out that the sales members were each feeling bruised and some were bitter because each of their former managers had decided they would be transferred to this new team, so they felt unappreciated and undervalued.

Officially, they knew I was their leader, but unofficially, several of them attempted to undermine my leadership during the first six months of the new division formation. I had my work cut out for me, but within one year, they appreciated more revenue growth than any other sales team in the company. I attribute much of their success to the unofficial leadership benefits I had gained over time.

Two years later, I would report to a new manager who was eager to find out from my staff about my leadership, and she poked around asking staff various questions about me. That manager and I later became great friends, which we are still to this day. She told me that never before had she been so impressed with the loyalty she witnessed from various employees who reported to me. Her words were that "each of them will take a bullet for you if necessary, and I am curious as to how you accomplished that." I told her that what I do is simply take great care of people. She probed further, about what that meant. I told her about my leadership character, which are the principals I believe in as a leader and are based upon the foundation of doing business responsibly, respectfully, and with integrity.

I believe that great leaders deliver results and are driven, often requiring more of themselves than what others actually expect. I told her about several examples of having directly demonstrated to my staff how I had their best interest in mind and at heart. I created cohesiveness within the team by encouraging and allowing them to participate in decisions that would affect us. I was a part of the "us," so they knew I was an active team player, which encouraged them to act similarly. Lastly, I kept myself open and honest as to my weaknesses by allowing my team and colleagues to give me feedback regarding my performance. All of these practices and others seem to thrust me forward in performance, but more importantly, I grew personally, which ultimately affected my professional growth. Although my role was official, they respected me more each time I demonstrated that I was unapologetically proud of our unit—our team—by taking great care seeing that my team was well informed, prepared, trained, inspired, and rewarded. Therefore, they became the best performing sales team with the highest percentage of revenue growth year after year for several consecutive years. They sold for me what other managers could not sell. In short, I was able to inspire them to sell beyond that which they expected and that which others had expected from them previously.

Wright

What about leadership—did you learn from the opportunity to build a new team from an existing and somewhat disgruntled staff?

Cole

I learned much about myself and how I approach challenges. I realized that my attitude was always: Yes, I can do that. I learned that I am innovative because I created several new products in the portfolio, including *The Los Angeles Times*' "Kids Reading Page," which continues to be published currently. I never consider failing at whatever endeavor I undertake. I am persistent, authentic, sincere, respectful, and uncompromising on quality, all of which drives great leadership prowess.

Wright

What are five entrepreneurial leadership traits/abilities that are pivotal to successful leadership?

Cole

1. *Branding/Marketing*—Leaders must project a winning image for the role they play. Savvy leaders create a brand for themselves that people—whether they are employees, vendors, peer leaders, or customers—embrace. A solid brand message is

one that shows character that people believe, respect, embrace, and therefore will follow and/or buy.

2. *Solid Judgment*—Leaders must filter effectively to recognize those things that have priority and therefore must be executed. They have the capacity to decide or make independent judgment calls when necessary and as appropriate. Finally, they align adequate resources to execute the call(s). Strong leaders accept that it is they who define and direct the company and therefore carry the burden and blessings of outcomes independent of others.

3. *Well-rounded Strategic Thinking*—Successful leaders think strategically, and in most regards, globally. They have a keen sense of tactical appreciation for those who execute programs, policy, and processes from the front line. This ensures that they are empathically connected with all that is required to accomplish the goals and objectives in the management of the business. Therefore, they acknowledge and value the importance of the management role, while recognizing that such tactical activity is not the best use of their time. In other words, if someone else can do it, it should be delegated.

4. *Confident and Courageous*—Leaders are not timid or afraid to make the tough calls and can and will hang on during the tough and challenging periods (slow economy, downsizing staff, shortage of cash flow, etc). They expect short-term differences to emerge regularly during their pursuit of long-term goals and objectives. Therefore, they know how and when to adjust tactics and strategies seamlessly as they embrace uncertainty.

5. *Respectful*—Great leaders, who demonstrate respect in all levels of their interactions, create a culture of teamwork, collaboration, and partnership. Therefore, during times of conflict, criticism, low performance, undesirable market conditions, etc., true leaders maintain their professionalism, integrity, and principles, all of which are qualities of respect.

Wright

As you manage your business in a highly competitive industry in a market with several competitors, how do you as a great leader and other great leaders differentiate themselves from their competitors?

Cole

Differentiation is critical, regardless of the industry or market in which the business is occurring. If competing businesses offer the same or similar product lines, inventories, levels of customer service, pricing, etc., then potential customers have many options to choose, which lowers the demand and subsequent potential for profits, because whatever is being offered lacks uniqueness. The degree to which competitors can easily replicate whatever you are offering, especially if they can improve upon what you offer, is directly tied to the profit-earning potential of the business.

I am in the newspaper industry in what is considered a niche market—ethnic press. There are at least three other niche papers competing for the same dollars and with an overlap in our core group of readers in the marketplace. Although my publication was the last to enter the market, I am convinced I have the most loyal readership of the three papers in that market competing against *Our Weekly*.

My loyal readership is primarily driven by our abilities to create layers of differentiation on several fronts. We believe that if our readers perceive they can bypass reading *Our Weekly*, and instead read a competing paper and essentially have the same news product, then we are failing in a strategic area. This can ultimately serve as the beginning of our ending. Therefore, it is particularly deliberate that *Our Weekly* is a unique tabloid size, publishes provocative and edgy cover stories, produces more original news stories, historical pieces, and exclusive feature articles, and launched with a Web site that fully archives content unlike any other competing paper in the market. We also recognize that product differentiation also impacts performance. If the product is superior to competing products, it's a great beginning for the sales team.

Wright

How do market downturns or recessions affect leaders? Does behavior change?

Cole

Yes, our behavior will change to reflect the situation at hand. How dramatically different we force our product, internal operations, management skill-set, or the company (in general) is a factor of the market conditions we face. Take, for example, the economic woes that business owners faced during the recent recessionary market conditions of 2008 and 2009. Many businesses in my local area went under, some barely survived, while a few thrived during the period. In 2008, my business was significantly affected by shallow cash flow periods because many of my customers fought hard to manage through the crisis and reallocated their spending. As a consequence, they either cut back on advertising and marketing dollars or were slow to pay as their dollars dwindled.

In anticipation of a deeper cash flow effect that the economy was sure to have on my business in 2009, I began having specific mandatory strategy meetings with all employees, both in group sessions and individually in the fall of 2008. The big take-away I wanted all to leave with was the fact that 2009 would likely be the most challenging year of our five-year existence. And, as promised, 2009 was the most challenging year for *Our Weekly*. I specifically remember cautioning everyone, "If it's on your watch or under your domain, I expect you to get it, massage it, manage it, and see it through at the highest quality level possible. Now is not the time for any of you to look away from our business." I had a sense of urgency as it related to preparing to receive 2009, which I successfully transferred to the staff.

As a matter of fact, during this current recession, we decided that it represented a "perfect storm" opportunity in which to grow the business. Instead of hunkering down and riding out the storm, we leaned in and pressed forward during what most considered the worst economic downturn since the Great Depression. We expanded our product portfolio with the introduction of a new quarterly health-related magazine in April 2009, *Healthier You*, which distributes separately and differently from the newspapers.

In February 2010 we launched a new paper, *Our Weekly Antelope Valley*, to serve a burgeoning marketplace of readership, which was critically underserved in news and information specific to its 14 percent African American population. Additionally, in March 2010 we relaunched the *OurWeekly* Web site (see www.ourweekly.com), which positioned us to leverage the viral behavior of social media. In April 2010 we introduced a new stand-alone product, "Careers and Education," which was profitable at the outset.

As a business management graduate with a minor in economics, I learned that recessionary times often represent the greatest growth potential for business. It's a gutsy and risky move to force growth during a recession, but you learn to manage the fear and forge forward. Recessions force efficiencies that might otherwise not be as stringently committed. Cost-cutting measures during such periods is smart business. However, it is unwise to attempt to "save your way to prosperity" indefinitely. You've heard the saying, "You have to spend money to make money." Well, this certainly rings true as it relates to growing your business. Increasing spending to grow your business during a recession makes perfect sense, provided you are in a growth business, have a strong strategic plan, can dedicate appropriate resources to meet objectives of the plan, and can appreciate economies of scale. There are numerous benefits associated with such growth including better market and industry rates as demand drops in key areas, negotiable rates as vendors seek new business, and competitive advantage as you advance the game at a time when competitors are dead in the water, etc. Growing your business during recessionary times has the greatest upswing potential, and for some reason, it reminds me of the saying about banks—if you can prove to banks that you don't need money, you are in a better position to get money and similarly, if you can spend money at a time when others are dropping out of the market, it speaks volumes about your staying power.

Also, during the recession, I launched the Urban Media Foundation (UMF), a 501(c)(3), which is a program to educate, mentor, and advocate for inner-city youth who have an interest in journalism, media technology, mass communication, entrepreneurialism, and green initiatives. The offerings of the UMF program are unparalleled in the state of California. My vision for the program is to increase the diversity representation in mainstream media by exposing students to career opportunities available in the industry.

Wright

How important is it for managers/leaders to continue to learn new skills and information?

Cole

It is vitally important as leaders that we invest in ourselves by learning new skills, continuing our education, exposing ourselves to new ways of solving old problems, and having access to similarly situated leaders who bring unique perspectives to the table. Despite the fact that I believed I had a scarcity of time available to do much more than what I had already committed to, I decided to attend a workshop called the Business Technical Assistance Program (BTAP) during the fall of 2008 at UCLA Anderson School of Management, in the Harold and Pauline Price Center for Entrepreneurial Studies.

According to a UCLA Anderson School of Management press release, the BTAP initiative was developed and funded as a result of a collaborative effort of The Greenlining Institute and AT&T. The Greenlining Institute is a multiethnic public policy and advocacy think tank that advocates for low income and minority communities through economic development, consumer protection, health advocacy, campaign finance reform, civil rights, and leadership development. AT&T Inc. is one of the world's largest telecommunications holding companies and is the largest in the United States. AT&T companies are recognized as the leading worldwide providers of IP-based communications services to business and as leading U.S. providers of high speed DSL Internet, local, and long-distance voice, directory publishing, and advertising services. AT&T Inc. holds a 60 percent ownership interest in Cingular Wireless, which is the number one U.S. wireless services provider with 57.3 million wireless customers.

BTAP is led by the celebrated Dr. Alfred E. Osborne Jr., who is a senior associate dean and professor. According to its Web site, "BTAP is designed for entrepreneurs and/or executives in existing businesses who desire to develop their management skills to enhance their companies' revenues, profits, and market impact with an emphasis on technology. Traditionally, applicants have been in business for three to five years, have a minimum of $1,000,000 in revenues, and want to learn how to move their business to the next level." Making the call to attend was, by far, one of the best strategic decisions I made during the fall of 2008.

There were approximately twenty business owners who committed to attending the workshop all day Thursday through Sunday (what I initially considered grueling). In short, the session demanded that we think of those things we could do differently and determine exactly what was blocking attainment of goals and objectives, stifling performance, or marginalizing success in our businesses. I walked away with a concise strategic plan of initiatives with associated time lines. In retrospect, these plans fostered a higher level of overall performance for *Our Weekly* during 2009. Specifically, I identified several areas to cut cost, many of which I intended to implement in stages, and the last stage would affect people through lay-offs, if necessary. Now, I knew I could not expect to "save our way to prosperity" through the cost-cutting measures—I needed to also think about ways to grow revenue during the recession. A key critical take-away from the session was a new idea, which more than made the entire time investment worth it.

Wright

What was the idea?

Cole

One of the things I identified in our exercise as an obstacle to growth was the fact that a high ratio of businesses that my company depended on would be in financial turmoil and would either not pay for their advertisements, not advertise, or would be very slow to pay their bills. As the session forced me to think creatively, I almost stumbled across the thought, "What if I inspired a few of *Our Weekly's* higher revenue generating customers who have annual contracts with us to pay for their entire schedule in January?" I would inspire them through incentives I would offer (volume discounted rate, value added benefits, ease of process, etc.) I intended to develop a proposal to customers who spent significantly more than $100,000 annually. Therefore, I reasoned, if five or six of these customers were to say yes, my potential cash flow issue in 2009 would no longer pose a threat. And, for the most part, it worked. Not only did a few agree to the proposal, the checks came in before the end of January.

During the BTAP workshop, I realized that being there in a space that was dedicated to strategic thinking not only afforded me an opportunity to have the "quiet time" to think more creatively than when I am immersed in my daily grind, but it also allowed room for others to hear my challenges and offer their perspectives on how I might tackle the issue(s). There were numerous other invaluable lessons I took away that have been tried and tested at *Our Weekly*. My BTAP experience was one that reaffirmed, in my mind, the need for leaders to continue to develop personally while in the hunt to grow professionally.

Wright

You cut your teeth in the corporate arena of leadership, but you are now CEO of a company you co-founded five years ago. Has your leadership changed? What are the significant differences?

Cole

I believe that I have made subtle changes in leadership. In corporate, I had the great blessing and responsibility to oversee a division with an annual revenue portfolio of approximately $100 million. I had both an annual revenue and expense budget to manage. I had more than three hundred employees, several managers, supervisors, and eight regional offices in my organization. Because I had proven myself to have great judgment, balanced decisions, and was performance driven, my managers recognized that they could learn from me and tried to stay out of my way so I could grow my business—their business—for them. Therefore, in the latter part of my corporate career, I was, in fact, running my own business within the corporation for which I worked. At that time, I considered only 10 to 15 percent of my business out of my control because it was more influenced at the corporate-administration level. In retrospect, maybe I only had 60 to 75 percent control, but I approached my business with fewer self-conceived limitations about what I could or could not do. The significant differences between corporate leadership versus entrepreneurship (and this list is not exhaustive) are that entrepreneurs have more autonomy, can expedite change, are forced to be more efficient, have fewer economies of scale, and less funding, but they trade off for better control of organization culture.

Wright

Today we have been talking to Natalie Cole. She is CEO of *Our Weekly*, the largest circulating black-owned newspaper in Southern California. She is a no-nonsense innovative and creative leader, and *The Los Angeles Times'* "Kids Reading Page" was her brainchild.

Natalie Cole's career, having spanned three decades, much of it at senior levels in a Fortune 500 company, revealed her to be an undeniably classic entrepreneur waiting to be freed from the constraints of corporate life.

As general market media papers lost market share and consolidated, the newspaper veteran noticed an emerging niche market prospect in ethnic press. For fun, she developed a business plan to launch an ethnic community newspaper, and upon its completion, realized she had a viable business opportunity worth pursuing. She did just that.

Today, Cole is CEO and Publisher of Our Weekly, LLC, which she co-founded in September 2004. As CEO, she focuses on attaining breakaway results in key areas of the organization, which ensures its overall continual success while delivering unparalleled product quality. Our Weekly consists of two publications—Our Weekly Los Angeles and Our Weekly Antelope Valley, as well as a quarterly health magazine, Healthier You.

Our Weekly is the largest audited-circulation Black-owned newspaper in Southern California.

In 2007, Cole founded the Urban Media Foundation (UMF) for which she serves as CEO. UMF is a non-profit afterschool program for underserved inner-city youth in Los Angeles who have an interest in media and its associated technology, communications, professional development, entrepreneurialism, financial literacy, and green initiatives.

In addition to UMF, Cole's philanthropic outreach efforts include serving or having served on numerous boards. She has served as a director with the National Association of Women Business Owners, Los Angeles Chapter, a director with the United Negro College Fund, an officer with National Newspaper Publishers Association, chair of Urban Media Foundation, and Commissioner of Information Technology and Commissioner for Community Redevelopment Agency with the City of Los Angeles.

Because of her vast life and career experiences, Cole lectures and presents on the following subjects: entrepreneurialism, media, women in business, establishing a not-for-profit, leadership, management, mentorship of youth and women, marketing, and advertising.

Natalie Cole

Our Weekly, LLC
8732 S. Western Avenue
Los Angeles, CA 90047
323-905-1301
ncole@ourweekly.com
www.ourweekly.com
www.urbanmediafoundation.org

CHAPTER 4

Your Image Matters! Use it to Powerfully Market Your Personal Brand

by Kathryn Lowell

THE INTERVIEW

David Wright (Wright)

Today we're talking with Kathryn Lowell. When Kathryn, Founder of Image Matters, graduated from Yale University and started working on Wall Street, she quickly discovered a key to success that was never taught in school—a polished personal image. Throughout her professional career in finance, emerging market development, and as an entrepreneur, she studied the attributes of a personal image that set apart the highest achievers. In 2001, she launched Image Matters, Inc. to advise corporate groups and individuals alike on image enhancement as a steppingstone to higher productivity, effective leadership, and personal success. For hundreds of individual clients, and for audiences at her popular talks and seminars, she is a trusted expert who demystifies the complexities of wardrobe, grooming, business and social etiquette, interpersonal behavior, and effective public speaking.

Kathryn delivers easy to understand principles that take people from ordinary to outstanding and from career stagnation to career acceleration. With an MBA in finance and entrepreneurship from UCLA and corporate experience in the United States and in Europe, she is uniquely qualified to address the personal image needs of employees at all levels of an organization. Her specialty is assisting career climbers achieve the qualities of executive presence. As a Certified Image Professional through the Association of Image Consultants International, she is one of only one hundred and thirty individuals worldwide with this high level designation.

Kathryn Lowell, welcome to *Yes You Can!*

Kathryn Lowell (Lowell)

Thank you, David; it's a pleasure to be a part of this project.

Wright

So what is your definition of personal image?

Lowell

David, if I have to sum it up, our image is how other people experience us. We are like a multimedia experience to the people we meet. More than a photograph or a resume or a set of accomplishments, we are experienced multidimensionally at the first encounter and continually at each subsequent encounter. People experience us in three general ways: how we look, how we act, and how we sound. In fact, in the image consulting industry, we call these categories the ABC's: Appearance, Behavior, and Communication.

Now, within these categories, there are literally dozens of components. For example, when we consider appearance, we obviously think generally about wardrobe and grooming but within those two categories there are many elements to consider such as style of clothes, appropriate colors or patterns, fabrics, shoes, accessories, undergarments, hair style, etc. Then, considering our behavior (or how we act) there are still many other aspects of image to consider—body language, use of gestures, posture, stance, eye contact, the ability to give a good handshake, and so on. How we communicate involves our vocal image and all the qualities of our voice that affect how people experience us. This includes our tone, the emotion in our voice, the range of our vocabulary, our volume and pitch, proper use of grammar, as well as our ability to speak to groups.

So actually, when considering the personal image of my clients, I compare it to a jigsaw puzzle with many, many different pieces. My goal is to get each of the pieces in place so the result is an image that is confident, powerful, and effective. I'm aiming to increase the charisma of my clients—both in their professional and social settings. When the pieces of the image puzzle are in place, we create a remarkable two-part result. First, my clients feel and act much more confident and attractive. And second, they are treated with much more respect from everyone they meet.

There is another way to think about our personal image and that is by comparing it to the idea of a brand, such as a corporate brand or even a product brand. There are two things that are crucial for a brand (and likewise your image) to become well known and valuable.

First of all, a brand should be *highly identifiable*. Think, for example, about the Coca-Cola brand. The curved shape of the original Coke bottle has practically become synonymous with the product itself. The color on the containers, the logo, and even the font of the logo are elements that have made the Coke brand highly recognizable all over the world, even when the words themselves are in foreign languages. Companies spend a great deal of time and resources to create product packaging that is memorable and highly recognizable. Likewise, we can become highly recognizable and increase the value of our own brand by working on and improving our own "packaging" through our attire, our grooming, and our actions.

The second crucial element for a strong and valuable brand is *consistency*. When a brand consistently delivers a service or experience with a high level of quality, consumers trust it and know they can depend on the brand over time.

So let's think again about the Coke brand. No matter where you are in the world, when you open a Coke, you know that you'll hear that same effervescent fizz. You know that the product inside will be the same refreshing beverage that you've counted on many times in the past. The Coke "experience" has been extremely consistent.

The very same principles apply to our image. When we are highly recognizable through our "packaging," and if we provide the same consistent positive experience through how we look, sound, and act, we increase the value of our image—we increase the value of our own personal brand.

Wright

In these casual times is our image really that important anymore?

Lowell

Actually, David, upgrading and maintaining our personal image is crucially important in unpredictable economic times such as those we're experiencing right now in this country. Our personal image is the key factor in marketing ourselves. A strong personal image can be our strategic advantage to gaining employment, getting faster promotions, making more and better social and professional contacts, and ultimately making more money. This is possible precisely because of how casual and complacent almost everyone has become about his or her image. The cultural messages around us seem to indicate that "anything goes" with regard to how we dress, act, and speak. As a result, Americans have become increasingly sloppy and careless—not only in appearance, but in the way we communicate and how we treat each other. While this is an unfortunate reality, the current situation also provides a great opportunity for us to stand out from the crowd. For the individual who becomes more self-aware and takes the steps to improve his or her image, real benefits will follow. The person who pays attention to his or her personal image will become the obvious person to be hired, to be promoted, to be sought as a mate (if that's what is being sought), and to be followed as a leader. Bucking the casualness of our culture holds real value for us these days, because it sets us apart, makes us more credible, and more worthy of respect.

Wright

What holds people back from maximizing the potential of their personal image?

Lowell

As I've alluded to, many people simply lack self-awareness. In my seminars and classes, my first task is to make my audiences aware of the influence of image and how vital it is to upgrade, maintain, and monitor one's own personal brand, and to understand that a strong personal image is a crucial and valuable asset in business. Education, experience, and know-how are the foundations of a great career, but without a strong personal image, we will never achieve our full potential.

I have seen too many people invest time and money in education and, frankly, still come up short in their careers because they lack certain image elements. Individuals pay a big price by ignoring or neglecting their image. By neglecting our image, we pay a tax—it may be a tax that we are not even aware of but it certainly exists and it's costing us dearly. This tax prevents us from capitalizing on certain opportunities, forging better relationships, or progressing in our career. Why is this so? Why don't people use their image effectively? In my work I have found quite a number of common reasons why people don't manage their own image better—let me give you a few.

First, many of us are simply unaware of the image expectations required for a particular position or career. This happens because most students graduating from high school or college have never had a class on image or etiquette or professionalism. Fewer companies than ever have a clearly defined or enforced dress code. Excellent role models for appearance and behavior are increasingly rare. Because most people do not receive the image training or feedback prior to being hired or on the job, they simply don't know the key elements of a professional image.

Here is another one: many of us have never learned the fundamentals of wardrobe and grooming, body language, or verbal presentation skills. If, for example, I didn't grow up in a family that valued good dining etiquette, chances are I may never have learned how to properly handle myself at an important dinner or reception. If I didn't take a speech class in high school or classes that required presentations in college, I may never have learned the skills for public speaking that are so important for professional advancement. So often we simply missed learning the fundamentals of image or we didn't have good role models to emulate, and our ignorance of what to do is holding us back.

Another barrier that keeps people from maximizing the value of their image is their own attitude. For example, I often hear people say that personal image no longer matters in today's society or that it's only their skill set that is important. There are also misconceptions about what it takes to create a good image. Some people I meet say it costs too much to maintain a good image. Frankly, in my opinion, this couldn't be more false. When necessary I have outfitted individuals in professionally appropriate clothing purchased from thrift shops for a small price. Other aspects of image are essentially free. Many books are available from the public library that can equip us with the skills for effective communication and interpersonal behavior. The information is out there, so ignorance is no excuse.

Finally, I meet people who claim to know what to do, but they complain about not having enough time. We're all pressed for time, so to me this is simply another way of saying that they haven't prioritized image issues in their lives. Your image can only become powerful when you set high standards for the way you present yourself and when you insist on being consistent.

Wright

So how important is the first impression?

Lowell

In my industry, we used to talk about our first impression occurring within three to five seconds. Within that short period of time, people form a variety of opinions about us based on what they see. However, findings from a Princeton University study published in 2006 really surprised me about how quickly humans form a first impression. In that study it was found that for five traits—attractiveness, likeability, trustworthiness, competence, and aggressiveness—we humans form opinions and make judgments in one tenth of a second. This means that humans form an opinion about these five traits in a fraction of a second—that's shockingly fast. So if we form conscious or unconscious opinions about these character traits after a split second of exposure to a face, imagine all the other opinions we rapidly form upon observing more than just a person's face such as clothes, grooming, actions, and so forth.

In addition to the unbelievably quick judgments rendered during the first impression, psychologists also tell us that the first impression is extremely strong and remarkably long-lasting. Consider that when we initially meet someone, the few minutes we spend in that first encounter may only represent a tiny portion of our entire life. However, to the person we meet, those few minutes represent all he or she knows about us—it's the totality of his or her experience with us, and this is a powerful notion.

Part of the power of the first impression is that there exists this unique moment in time. Because we have the opportunity to use those first seconds to our best advantage, it makes sense that we maximize every good quality we have during that first encounter with anyone we meet. We need to pull out all the stops, making sure our visual image is excellent, our handshake is perfected, our introductory words friendly and clear, and our body language open and confident.

We have, at that moment, the ability to create a "halo effect." The halo effect is an expression psychologists use to describe our tendency to extend a good overall impression based on one good first encounter. In other words, in our image bank, we receive extra credit from others when we make a good first impression, and that extra credit lingers and influences subsequent encounters until we do something to undermine that favorable impression. This is a powerful idea that we can use to our advantage.

Wright

So what are the key factors of the visual aspect of our image?

Lowell

Let me answer that in the context of the all important first impression I was just explaining. When we initially meet someone as he or she approaches, obviously the very first thing we notice is clothing. Because clothing covers most of the body and it looms large in our field of vision, we pick up multiple clues about someone's image through the messages that the clothing the person is wearing send us. For example, we make judgments about someone's level of success by seeing the quality of his or her garments, and we judge the person's attention to detail by observing the condition of his or her shoes. Rightly or wrongly we may ascribe a measure of a person's self-respect by checking his or her hygiene and grooming. If the person's clothes, accessories, or hairstyle are out of date, we might even predict that the person's business knowledge or skills may be out of date. If the person's attire is overly trendy it may call into question his or her maturity.

I like to talk about clothes first because our wardrobe is an image element that we can easily change and upgrade. But let me also address the cultural standard of attractiveness as defined by qualities such as body shape, facial symmetry, feature proportionality, height, muscularity for men, breast to waist to hip proportions for women, healthy looking skin and hair, etc. We know from many studies that there exists a cultural bias favoring people that have features of attractiveness or beauty. In other words, these people tend to have an easier time making a great first impression and are generally offered more social advantages throughout their life, although their looks do not guarantee success.

But here is the ironic truth of attractiveness and image: a good personal image has less to do with beauty and much more to do with likeability. Many of us feel that if we're not beautiful by the standards I previously mentioned then we aren't attractive and therefore we don't have a good image. But guess what—very few people actually live up to those

Hollywood standards of beauty. Only a small fraction of the population qualifies as beautiful in those terms. The reality is that anyone, and I really mean *anyone,* can take the steps to become attractive and likeable by being well-dressed, well-groomed, smiling, displaying confidence and kindness, speaking with eloquence and conviction, and always adhering to the highest standards of civility and integrity. When you have these qualities, you have likeability, and when you have likeability, you are attractive.

Wright

You also mention vocal or verbal image. Would you explain what you mean?

Lowell

In image terms, our voice is our second face. Many people underestimate the influence of vocal qualities to define their credibility and professionalism. For example, we can demonstrate confidence by projecting our voice to fill a room and by eliminating filler words. Filler words such as "um," "ah," " like," and "sort of" are words that don't add anything to our speech and can immediately undermine the perception of our intelligence or make us seem insecure. Eliminating filler words can be a huge boost to the vocal image of professionals I meet. Sometimes they're used so unconsciously that they are a blind spot dragging down my clients' image. Eliminating filler words is a quick and easy way to improve your vocal image.

We can also project a friendly image with a warm, well-modulated tone that is positive. People who are perceived as secure and successful have that ability to come across as warm and dynamic at the same time. We can project an image that is passionate and upbeat by speaking with energy and enthusiasm, by varying our speech patterns, and by keeping out of the monotone range. We can also demonstrate sensitivity in our business dealings by avoiding jargon or buzz words that exclude others. And we can develop an image of intelligence and clarity by developing a robust vocabulary that allows full expression of our ideas.

Ultimately, I want all my clients to be confident public speakers. Their professional image will be incomplete if they do not face the reality of their effectiveness in front of groups. Like many people, I put off facing my fears and insecurities about public speaking until my mid-thirties and I'm sure it cost me at various times in my career.

It's never too late, however, to get the training and practice needed to deliver effective presentations, whether to a group of two or two thousand. And you don't need expensive training to become an outstanding speaker. Your local Toastmasters club is an ideal place to start this process. At Toastmasters, in civic or social clubs, or at church events, you can experiment with your delivery style until you find your authentic voice without the pressure of an on-the-job presentation. It is also imperative to record and listen to yourself. Once you get past the "ugh, is that really how I sound?" reaction, you can focus on improving your vocal qualities and eliminate any weaknesses.

Wright

How does nonverbal body language factor in creating a strong personal image?

Lowell

We all have the ability to speak without opening our mouths. Our nonverbal presence sends so many messages to the people around us, and it consists of elements such as how we move our body, how we gesture, how we orient ourselves toward others, our facial expressions, as well as our posture and our stance. Even involuntary actions like our blink rate, our pupil dilation, and our blushing reaction send loud messages about our emotional state. If you don't know the fundamentals of nonverbal messages, you are definitely at a professional and social disadvantage.

As professionals, we must understand nonverbal communication from three perspectives: 1) Managing the messages we are sending to others, 2) Interpreting the messages others are sending out, and 3) For those professionals who travel abroad or interact with people from other cultures, understanding and interpreting differences in eye contact, personal space issues, touch frequency, and insult gestures that might offend our foreign business contacts.

Generally, as businesspeople, we want to convey body language that is secure and confident. We can achieve this with a good posture, a firm and dry handshake, direct eye contact, keeping our hands away from our head and face, and maintaining a neutral stance with hands out of pockets and not clasped in front of us. We also want to exhibit a professional presence that is approachable and friendly. We can achieve this with appropriate smiling (that's *genuine* smiling, not a false grin), keeping our legs and arms open and uncrossed and our hands relaxed. We can show respect and honor to others by orienting our bodies to fully face them, leaning in to show our interest and nodding to encourage their participation in a conversation.

The ability to interpret body language—both larger body gestures and the microexpressions that flash across the face in an instant—is a skill that businesspeople must develop. Reading the body and the face of our boss, our client, or our colleagues gives us added insight to manage business situations. Speakers, for example, must constantly "take the temperature" of their audience by watching for reactions throughout a presentation. Telltale signs that the crowd is losing interest occur when audience members look down, touch their face, head or hair, lean back, cross arms, flip through notes or handouts, fidget, or have a glazed over stare. On the other hand, an audience that is tuned in watches the speaker and listens intently, with only minimal breaks in eye contact. Some audience members will nod and smile, providing encouraging feedback for engaging speakers. Watching for changes in the audience's mood by observing nonverbal cues can give a seasoned speaker the opportunity to adjust the content or delivery style. Likewise, we can use our knowledge of the nonverbal to adapt and respond to changing situations in our business environment.

Wright

Are there other aspects of image that people should understand?

Lowell

Yes. In times past, our first impression and initial image began when people met us in person. However, in today's Internet society, our online image precedes our in-person image. It has become more difficult to maintain a private identity that is distinct from our public image. Almost everyone has access to Google, Facebook, and other applications that can be used to search and reveal every bit of our personal life and history. Anything that we've ever posted online becomes instantly accessible to millions of others, and it's only with difficulty that we can expunge material that has been released into the Internet. Employers now routinely search online for information about applicants. Any comments, blogs, or pictures that we might have innocently posted for fun or in jest can be then scrutinized in a negative light.

How we use the Internet can also affect our image. Consider someone who comments incessantly on Facebook. After a while you might start to wonder about this person, "Doesn't he [or she] have a life?" So even the amount of time we spend online commenting on Facebook or Tweeting can give the impression that we may not be utilizing our time effectively or, after one too many mundane comments, that we are just boring.

Just yesterday, one of my friends (a small business owner) told me that a recent hire writes foul language on her Facebook page. Her immediate reaction was one of distrust and she said, "I'll never feel the same way about this person again. I feel like she's demonstrating poor judgment and I interpret that as a character flaw." Wow! While the freedom of expression the Internet offers is attractive, there is also a real life price to pay if what we post damages our image and professional brand.

Wright

So what are some of the common blind spots or bad habits that you most often encounter with your clients?

Lowell

Wow, there are just so many areas in which the people I meet have little or no self-awareness that it's challenging to just pick out two or three examples. I've already talked about the first impression—most of us understand we should make an effort to create a good first impression. However, a good first impression must be backed up with consistency. Consistently being well-dressed, well-presented, well-spoken, and well-mannered makes our image strong and valuable. So this is a huge blind spot for many people. They may know what to do, but they have simply become too relaxed and too complacent and their image suffers as a result.

Let me give you some typical examples. For my women clients, I almost always see an opportunity to immediately upgrade their image with an excellent hairstyle and by setting *regular* hair appointments to keep it looking good. Hair is an area where women can do too much or too little and get similarly poor results. So while I advise most women to cover their gray, I suggest restraint from too much processing. I recommend avoiding too much highlighting or unusual coloring if it distracts from your face, and definitely switching stylists if they're not delivering a cut that suits your face and suits your professional needs.

For men, an example of a common blind spot I see in my geographic region is wearing a dress shirt with the top button open to reveal a T-shirt underneath. A T-shirt, in this case, is *underwear* and underwear should not be visible. Therefore, I always recommend that men buy v-neck, not crew neck, undershirts. Certainly, a lack of attention to the fit and quality of their clothes is a huge blind spot for many of my clients. I almost always introduce clients to a skilled tailor who can provide alterations to garments that may not fit perfectly "off the rack." I also encourage my clients to see the value of "less is more" by purchasing fewer, but better quality items that will last and enhance their visual image.

For high achieving young professionals, I also see weaknesses in etiquette knowledge, especially dining etiquette. This is perhaps a symptom of our fast food culture, or the lack of family time around the dinner table, but I am amazed by the level of ignorance of even basic dining skills, such the proper way to hold and use utensils or understand the table setting elements. Such basics as offering a good handshake or speaking clearly are frequent blind spots I see in the arena of behavior and communicating. As part of my image consulting practice, I offer an online self-assessment for clients to evaluate their own image strengths, weaknesses, and blind spots. I'm happy to direct the readers to this great tool—just send me an e-mail requesting the Professional Image Self-Assessment.

Wright

What image challenges do you see among the generations in today's corporate workplace?

Lowell

With four generations sharing today's corporate offices, there are inevitable differences and even clashes between the groups based on their particular traits and values that define each and that were formed by the times in which they grew up. Clearly, one of the issues that cuts cleanly between the older groups of the Traditionalists and the Baby Boomers versus the younger generations—Gen X and Gen Y—is their comfort with and use of technology. While the younger groups are experts of all things digital, especially social media, texting, and tweeting, they are generally weaker in face-to-face communications, reading and responding to nonverbal cues, and many other areas of interpersonal social interaction and public speaking.

Having grown up with the immediacy of information as well as having been programmed with multiple activities in their youth, Gen X and Gen Y have the reputation as higher maintenance and less patient employees. While the idea of paying one's dues is so familiar to the Traditionalists and older Baby Boomers, the younger generations are much less likely to wait around for advancement.

With Gen Y in particular, the ability of celebrities to influence their grooming and attire has created a definite void in understanding the appropriate corporate dress and grooming that will help them with the advancement they crave. For the Traditionalists and older Baby Boomers, the corporate landscape has evolved dramatically during their own careers such that now the image pressure they face is to be as relevant, as current, and as vigorous as possible in order to be respected by their younger colleagues. For these veterans of the workforce who may be unwilling to adapt, they must ask themselves, "Am I aging well or am I stuck in another era?"

Another priority for older workers is to understand and adopt the latest technology. They also must be able to keep up with the physical demands of their job, as the pace of business life has accelerated just as their own bodies are starting to slow down. This means they must maintain their physical fitness and health to meet the business schedules, longer days, and travel requirements of today. Of course, maintaining and upgrading their wardrobe and grooming are critical to avoid being typecast as the "old guy," or the "old woman" in the office.

In contrast, members of Gen Y (or Millennials) face big challenges with a wardrobe of jeans and flip-flops and a proliferation of tattoos and body piercings that are abhorrent to their older managers. So think twice before getting that body art on your spring break beach trip. It might end up being a permanent reminder of a momentary lapse of judgment. And, as a caution to women of all generations, in the words of one of my image industry colleagues, "The more skin you show, the more opportunities you blow."

Wright

So what are two or three things that people should work on every day to improve their image?

Lowell

First, never leave the house without checking yourself in a full-length mirror and asking, "Do I look like a professional?" "Does my wardrobe and grooming truly give the impression that I am ready to get the job done?" I recommend bucking the casual trend by establishing a clear level of dress below which you personally refuse to go. This level will be uniquely defined by your industry, your own corporate environment, and your own career aspirations. But, let's say you decide today that you simply will no longer wear jeans to work (which, by the way, I think is a great guideline for most corporate career climbers). This "no jeans policy" becomes your new personal standard, so that no matter what everyone else is doing you will stick to this one rule, which will help you be consistent in your visual presentation.

Now, another thing you can do to improve your image is to talk to someone new every single day. Most of us have a set pattern to our day that is very familiar and comfortable—we do the same things day in and day out. I recommend that you push outside the norm and find ways to interact with new people. This will keep your communication skills—both nonverbal and verbal—fresh and agile.

As I mentioned previously, I recommend that everyone find a way to practice speaking in front of groups in order to gain a comfort level there. Too many people languish in their careers because they have some weakness in the area of public speaking.

Another way to improve your image is to find opportunities to demonstrate civility and be socially generous each day. Make time for conversation—ask questions, show a desire to help others. Not only will these actions make you more likable, but you'll find ways to practice the skills that demonstrate confidence. This comes easily to some people, but for many of us it is a stretch. It's only by stretching that we will grow.

Wright

So who hires an image consultant—and why?

Lowell

You might meet with an image consultant for any number of reasons. Many of my own clients are professionals who wish to maximize their professional credibility. "Developing executive presence" is a buzz phrase that has received a lot of press lately, but this is essentially what I've been doing with clients for nearly a decade. A certified image consultant with significant experience can help bring into sharp focus the image issues that may have been holding you back or that you may have been avoiding, and will provide a reasonable plan of action for upgrading appearance, behavior, and communication skills. As an objective third party, an image coach will tell you the truth in a constructive way, even when your own loved ones may have been trying to tell you the same thing for years and you haven't listened. Taking the emotional connection out of the relationship really helps my clients, especially when I help them see what tangible results image improvement can achieve.

Another group of individuals who can benefit from the counsel of an image consultant are those seeking to enter the workforce for the first time, such as college graduates or those returning to the job market, such as parents who have taken time away from their previous employment to raise their kids. And, of course, anyone who has been downsized or has otherwise lost a job can benefit from the objective advice and encouragement that an image professional can provide.

As far as working with image professionals, two things are really important. First, find a consultant with whom you have a good chemistry. In other words, make sure your personalities are a good match so that you trust the consultant and will act on his or her suggestions. Second, ensure that the consultant with whom you choose to work has the correct specialty knowledge or experience to work on your needs.

Many people in our industry focus on a particular niche. Some, for example, may just work with one gender or, possibly even more specifically, just work on wardrobe for women. Others may specialize in color analysis, while others may focus exclusively on corporate group training and do less one-on-one work with individuals. Others may have less to do with appearance, but are more focused on communication skills or on corporate etiquette.

Wright

What a great conversation and one that is timely for me since I'm hiring right now. I'm so surprised by the way people look when they walk into the office, and I'm even more surprised by some of the things they say.

Lowell

It really is surprising, isn't it? In my business, I serve people from all walks of life—from teens to senior citizens—because everybody can use help in one way or another and we all have at least a couple of blind spots. However, I tend to focus primarily on corporate professionals by providing both group training sessions and one-on-one consultations. Within this demographic, I work on all areas of professional and executive presence from wardrobe to grooming to vocal presence and body language.

At my company's office we offer many services ranging from interview skills to presentation training with video playback to private makeup tutorials. We also offer high-end wardrobe options shown privately to our clients. I also go to clients' homes to help them with wardrobe management and teach them how to shop effectively. I draw on many outside resources such as tailors, hairstylists, nutritionists, dentists, even acting as my clients' advocate if they're considering cosmetic procedures. Some of my coaching is conducted via webcam for those with whom I cannot meet face-toface, and this works remarkably well.

The relationship I develop with clients is very unique, as I become a trusted insider to their lives. Because no two people have the same exact set of image issues, my goal is to meet each person where he or she is with regard to the person's own authentic self. I help my clients maintain their individuality and comfort while amplifying more positive image qualities.

The main reason why I do this work is because of the amazing results I've witnessed when people start their image improvement. I have seen clients offered excellent career promotions and rise to the very top of their industry. They are able to influence their colleagues in new and effective ways, attract the mate of their dreams, and most importantly, gain more personal respect and dignity by turning on a more powerful and dynamic presence.

Wright

Well, Kathryn, this has been a great conversation. I really appreciate all this time you've taken with me to answer these questions. I have learned a lot here today and I am certain that our readers will too.

Lowell

Thanks so much, David. It's been a pleasure.

Wright

Today we've been talking with Kathryn Lowell, graduate of Yale University and founder of Image Matters, Inc. Kathryn helps corporate groups and individuals craft a polished and effective personal and professional image that brings them more respect and credibility. Her specialty is assisting career climbers achieve the qualities of executive presence.

Kathryn, thank you so much for being with us today on *Yes You Can!*

Lowell

Thanks again.

When Kathryn Lowell, Founder of Image Matters, graduated from Yale University and started working on Wall Street, she quickly discovered a key to success that was never taught in school—a polished personal image. Throughout her professional career in finance, emerging market development, and as an entrepreneur, she studied the attributes of a personal image that set apart the highest achievers. In 2001, she launched Image Matters, Inc. to advise corporate groups and individuals alike on image enhancement as a steppingstone to higher productivity, effective leadership, and personal success. For hundreds of individual clients, and for audiences at her popular talks and seminars, she is a trusted expert who demystifies the complexities of wardrobe, grooming, business, social etiquette, interpersonal behavior, and effective public speaking.

Kathryn delivers easy to understand principles that take people from ordinary to outstanding and from career stagnation to career acceleration. With an MBA in finance and entrepreneurship from UCLA and corporate experience in the United States and in Europe, she is uniquely qualified to address the personal image needs of employees at all levels of an organization. Her specialty is assisting career climbers achieve the qualities of executive presence. As a Certified Image Professional through the Association of Image Consultants International, she is one of only one hundred and thirty individuals worldwide with this high level designation.

Kathryn Lowell

Image Matters, Inc.
309 S. Main Street
Bentonville, AR
479-271-2134
kathryn@imagemattersgroup.com
www.imagemattersgroup.com

CHAPTER 5

Opportunity Never Knocks: The Power of Innovative Leadership

by Dr. Howard Rasheed

THE INTERVIEW

David Wright (Wright)

Today we're talking with Dr. Howard Rasheed who writes and speaks on how to effectively accelerate innovation in organizations. Internationally known as the "Innovation Strategist," Dr. Rasheed is a coach and trainer for empowering innovation champions in their search for competitiveness. His upcoming book, *Reinvent Your Business Model: 7 Steps to Sustainable Innovation,* presents a simple but colorful metaphor of a strategic ecosystem for sustainable innovation. This science-based approach to innovation guides you to a renewable source of creative energy and transformational ideas. He has developed a proprietary system and software for innovating and ideation called "The Idea Accelerator." This science-based system has been used in applications for strategic transformation, think tanks, technology commercialization, and product development projects.

Dr. Rasheed is an Associate Professor of Strategy and Innovation at the University of North Carolina in Wilmington and Founder of the Institute for Innovation. He received his PhD in Global Strategic Management from Florida State University.

Dr. Rasheed, welcome to *Yes You Can!*

Howard Rasheed (Rasheed)

Thank you very much, David, and it's a pleasure to be here.

Wright

So what do you mean by the title "Opportunity Never Knocks"?

Rasheed

You've heard the old adage that opportunity never knocks twice; well, I'm a believer that opportunity never knocks at all. You have to go out and find opportunity—it does not seek you out. To use a quote by Thomas Edison, "Opportunity is missed by most people because it's dressed in overhauls and looks like work." We either avoid or simply do not see opportunities when they're presented.

We've also heard the statement that "luck is preparation meeting opportunity." So we want to take the approach of being proactive when it comes to opportunity. Since opportunity doesn't knock, we've got to go out and find it in order to achieve our human potential.

Wright

So how important is innovation in today's global economy?

Rasheed

Innovation has become a competitive imperative. The new mandate is innovate or perish. Research and development (R&D) spending on innovation is starting to decline in the United States. This is not just an issue of technology, but it's an issue that affects our quality of life and homeland security, according to a report on American competitiveness.

There are many disturbing trends in the United States. We find that technology savvy workers are starting to decline as a percentage of our population. We are starting to outsource a lot more of our R&D efforts offshore. Since technology-related revenue is almost half of our international trade surplus, this is a very important issue. Unfortunately, it's starting to decline as a percentage of our global share of high tech output. It's gone from 31 percent in 1980 to less than 15 percent in 2005 and it is continuing to decline.

So that's why we find, in surveys by some of the leading consulting firms, that over 70 percent of top managers and CEOs are saying that innovation is one of their top three priorities for their company.

Wright

So what do you think is wrong with how innovation is approached in today's business world?

Rasheed

One of the key areas, David, is that we've confined innovation to the product and development department in our organizations. In order to maximize our potential, innovation should be approached holistically. In other words, it should go beyond product development and R&D. We should look for opportunities throughout our organizations for reinventing our business models, new product development, strategic planning, and business process improvement. In order to do that, we have to have a more creative mindset in our organizations. We cannot just leave innovation to the scientists and the engineers, but we must encourage an innovative and creative thinking process in all of the entrepreneurs, employees, managers, and stakeholders who are involved in value-creating activities.

In order to do that, David, we have to look at how we can make innovation and creativity more systematic. Right now, we leave it to the serendipitous chance and random occurrences of inspiration of a lone inventor. That is not the way proactive and world-class organizations should behave. Organizations should have a system for innovation, just like they have a system for every other value-creating activity and operation in their organization. This innovation system could apply to accounting, word processing, or scientific achievement. Why not have innovation systems in which we stimulate creativity, innovation, and strategic transformation on a continuous and consistent basis?

Wright

How does having an innovative mind contribute to maximizing one's human potential?

Rasheed

What differentiates leaders is their ability to create a vision and inspire people to follow it. But that requires a creative mind stimulated by innovative thinking. Unfortunately, too often we get into a routine or a habit of following along with the pack and not creating waves. In fact, that's how we were conditioned in kindergarten—to not make trouble, to get along, and to conform. Creative minds are typically nonconformist. So we have to take a closer look at how we develop the habits of creativity.

First, we look at creativity in terms of the capacity of the human mind. Creativity is the ability to use your imagination to develop new and original ideas or things and think of ways of dealing with difficult problems. In order to be more creative, you must have a more disciplined imagination because this leads to idea creation, which is basically the forming of new ideas. An individual's creative ability is determined by his or her intellectual ability, knowledge, and style of thinking, personality, motivation, and environment. But what keeps us from being more creative are sometimes the filters and barriers we have created in our own minds.

One of the things that distinguishes humans is an innate ability to think; we can all form images and thoughts that can lead to creativity. But when we create these mental models that sometimes form as barriers to our thinking, we limit our ability to solve problems, we stifle our reasoning, and we contribute to a difficult process in terms of decision-making. So what I suggest is taking a closer look at the whole creative process from a perspective I call the "Six I's" or the "Six Dimensions of Creativity."

1. *Imagination.* Imagination is your ability to visualize and form images and ideas in your mind. Knowledge and other environmental information stimulate the imagination so you can actualize new ideas.
2. *Inspiration.* Inspiration is the motivation for the human mind to be creative and to create new thoughts.
3. *Insight.* This is the ability to arrive at an understanding of information or knowledge. More specifically, how do you

process and identify relationships and behaviors within a certain model or context?

4. *Ideation.* This is the process of idea generation—creating new ideas or concepts.

5. *Ingenuity.* Ingenuity refers to the process of applying ideas to solve problems or meet challenges.

6. *Invention.* Invention is the process of actually creating something new by using your creativity and imagination to design something or to configure a new device or new process.

So that's what I call the Six I's that we have to focus on to be more creative.

Wright

What does research suggest about how we can improve our ability to innovate?

Rasheed

There is some interesting new research that has come out of the Northwestern University Magnetic Resonant Imaging (MRI) Center that suggests humans are naturally resistant to change. This resistance blocks our creativity and innovation. In order to encourage creativity, one of the things we need to do is to challenge a person's paradigm. A paradigm is a set of assumptions about the way people perceive the world. It is a way of explaining and filtering our external environment. All of us have some context or perception in terms of how we look at the world; in order for us to be creative, sometimes we have to challenge those assumptions.

For instance, most people use a computer. But why does it have to be a box? Why does it have to sit on a table and why does it have to have a screen? Those are assumptions based on our current thinking about computers. Why not have it implanted or why not have a virtual display that is imbedded in our glasses? So we have to challenge our paradigms or assumptions in order to be creative.

One of the other things that the neuroscience research suggests is that we need to provide new ways of stimulating our neurons. These are nerves in our brain that cause thoughts and ideas. But humans are naturally disposed to avoid new ideas because it generally provokes some physiological discomfort. We can improve our ability to innovate after learning from this research and coming up with some ways to prepare the mind to maximize innovative thinking.

Wright

So how do you prepare the mind to maximize innovative thinking?

Rasheed

One of the keys to innovative thinking is to create an effective cognitive system that can discipline your imagination. Although it is based on neuroscience research, some of the ways you can address that are very simple. One is the act of "paying attention." This is the cognitive process of selectively concentrating on one thing while ignoring all others. One technique is called "focused attention," which is your ability to respond to specific visual, auditory, or tactical stimuli. To put it simply, paying attention to one specific thing in a repeated pattern will allow you to stimulate neuron activity.

Another way to maximize innovative thinking is to force yourself to absorb new information. According to research, as we absorb or process new information, this actually creates new neuron pathways. You've heard the research that suggests we only use 10 percent of our brain. Wouldn't it be scary if we used twice that much—20 percent? Doesn't sound like a lot, but that would be doubling our capacity. The way to do that is to keep creating new neuron pathways by forcing ourselves to focus attention on new information.

In the work we do with organizations, we use the technique of graphic visualization. This is a very consistent way to focus your attention and to achieve what is called "attention density." This means being able to absorb a lot more information in a focused way. One common graphic visualization technique that everyone is familiar with is mind-mapping, where you're actually using visualization prototypes, like diagrams that represent words. We use this technique for brainstorming because it allows us to form a picture, thereby focusing attention. And, as you know, it is said that a picture is worth a thousand words. A lot more information can be processed by creating a picture around it because now our brain can capture that picture around those concepts.

Wright

It's a little scary to think that every upward step since the beginning of time has been made by using only 10 percent of mankind's potential.

Rasheed

It would be amazing what our human potential for achieving success could be if we used these simple techniques to stimulate an innovative mind.

Wright

So how can people overcome their natural resistance to new ideas?

Rasheed

We talked about the technique called Attention Density, the process where you have repeated and long-lasting focus on new information. This draws energy from the part of the brain that supports our intellectual function and gets us away from using the frontal lobe of our brain. In their research, Rock and Schwartz talk about the fact that we often lapse into habits based on our old mental models and that use the frontal lobe of our brain.

I'll give you an example, David. Have you ever gotten in your car after work and said, "I'm going home," and the next thing you know, you're at home and never thought about it again? Well, that's because your frontal lobe went into gear and you operated on memory. That's what is comfortable for us. We always talk about our "comfort zone;" well, when we get new information and we're forced to deal with new situations, it makes us very uncomfortable, we perspire, and we get nervous.

I know you're a master speaker, David, but what I've heard from master speakers is that we never get rid of those butterflies—we just train them to fly in formation. That is because we're outside of our comfort zone, but as long as we keep pushing that envelope, our brains expand and we keep firing off new neurons.

Recent research suggests that to offset Alzheimer's and dementia, you need to keep your mind active. So they're suggesting that older people use crossword puzzles or go to the university and continue their education to keep those brain cells working.

Wright

So how does innovation compare to the process of opportunity recognition for entrepreneurs?

Rasheed

Many entrepreneurs do not really understand the sequence of venture creation. A lot of times, an idea pops up in our mind but we really don't understand that, although innovation starts with a good idea, the idea must start with recognizing opportunity. If you don't have an opportunity, it may be an idea, but it may not be a successful idea. So sometimes we come up with the answer without going through a systemized process of looking at information, finding the opportunity, and then coming up with the best idea. We then design a business model for each idea, starting with their unique value proposition.

I'll give you an example: I think there should be an ice cream shop downtown on the river in Wilmington, North Carolina, because everybody likes ice cream. But have I done my homework to see if there is a trend toward more people eating ice cream? Maybe people are not eating ice cream because of health issues. Maybe there has been an increase in consumers choosing low fat alternatives. So you must look at the trends whether they're health conscious issues, dietary issues, or nutritional issues. Or there may be unfavorable economic trends. Maybe the population is moving away from downtown to another section of town. So in this case, we process the effects of multiple trends and look for the opportunity. We don't start with the answer and then go back and justify it. Entrepreneurs need to understand that if they process their venture creation ideation or idea creation by first doing their homework, then look for the opportunity, and then come up with the idea, they would be a lot more successful.

Wright

What are some of the prevailing thinking models?

Rasheed

We've done some research around how people think and found various thinking models. One traditional approach is linear thinking, which is the process of thought that follows a step-by-step progression in a predetermined sequential path. In other words, linear thinking is based on associative logic; we make connections based on our previous experience. For instance, how many times have you offered a totally new idea only to have someone say, "Oh, is that like so and so?" Instead of really evaluating the idea on its own worth, people try to associate it with something that they already know. Human nature tends to filter out new information using our internal database and catalog it based on our old information and old experiences. Using this associative thinking with old information and old experiences, we usually get what we already know because that's in our comfort zone. It's what we are used to, so it's data based on historical—not future—information. So we need to get beyond the associative thinking process.

Wright

So what are some of the personality styles of innovative thinkers?

Rasheed

There is some research related to how people innovate and process information. One of the key approaches is the Kirton Adaptor-Innovator (KAI) model. In the KAI model, people are scored on a scale from adaptive to innovative, based on their assessment tool.

Another instrument called Innovation Style Assessment uses four dimensions of innovative thinking profiles labeled visioning, experimenting, exploring, and modifying. This is based on your typical approach to problem-solving and idea creation.

People who score high in "visioning" provide the big picture and long-term direction for the organization or project. They focus on visions and goals, even if the path to get there is uncertain. Then there are the "experimenters" who provide methods and systems to take risk in stages. They get people to collaborate and become involved in decision-making by developing a process of planning and working together. Next, there is the "explorer." Explorers challenge accepted ways of seeing things and seek out novel approaches to problems. They deal with turbulent change through a sense of courage or adventure. Then there are people who are "modifiers." They are responsive to immediate needs and maximize available resources. They help facilitate short-term motivation of groups and they keep change relevant to their current need. Some styles are a combination of these four dimensions.

This is some of the new research about styles of innovation. Our work typically starts with this assessment in order to get a perspective on how we think, how we process information, and basically come up with a profile that helps us understand ourselves and allows us to create more effective teams in our organizations. This enables us to have a diversity of approaches and maximize potential in our organizations.

Wright

What kind of knowledge best stimulates innovative thinking?

Rasheed

Historically, we have classified knowledge as tacit or explicit—things that are in our heads and things that are on paper, respectively. In both cases that's historical information—things we already know. We help organizations focus on what we call "dynamic knowledge" to stimulate innovative thinking. Dynamic knowledge is information that has movement in a direction over a period of time. It is basically knowledge that is dynamic in the sense that it represents change in the environment.

To illustrate, I use the analogy of Wayne Gretzky, the legendary hockey player. When asked about the key to his success, he reportedly replied, "I skate to where the puck is going to be, not to where the puck is." That's the concept of dynamic knowledge—"skating to where the puck is going to be," not trying to "catch up with the puck." The puck is going one hundred miles per hour, no one skates that fast. So you have to anticipate where the puck is going unless you're going to wait until it comes to rest or someone else seizes on the opportunity.

In our methodology, we focus attention on dynamic and future-relevant knowledge. What is a better definition and what are some examples of dynamic knowledge? First of all, they're prevailing trends, emerging issues, and expert predictions. Prevailing trends are historical data that have some background and is moving forward. It can be up or down, but it is usually some movement or change, more or less, higher or lower. For example, there has been an X percent increase in Y over the last Z years. That's a quantified trend.

An emerging issue is something that has happened very recently but does not represent a historical data pattern. For example, there has been an increased emphasis on healthcare reform. We don't have a whole lot of historical data on it, but it's obviously something that has emerged and is very important in our society.

Then you have expert predictions. For example, experts predict that we're going to have some major coastal erosion in the next ten years because of global warming. But predictions are dependent upon the veracity of the data and the qualifications of the expert making the prediction. These are examples of dynamic knowledge. It is a group or set of information that has future-focused value and relevance to what we are trying to do.

Wright

What are visualization prototyping techniques and how do they stimulate innovative thinking?

Rasheed

The unique method we use for stimulating innovative thinking is a concept we call "Bisociation Brainstorming®." This is the process by which prevailing trends, emerging issues, expert predictions, and scenarios converge, interact, or intersect. What we have come to understand from research is that some of the more sensational ideas actually come from the convergence or the interaction of two or more trends. This concept was first suggested by Art Koestler in a book he wrote in 1964 called the *Act of Creation*. He suggested the most interesting ideas come from bisociation— the intersection of two different concepts. The more different or dissimilar they are, the more unexpected and impressive the discoveries can be. Johansson calls it the Medici Effect.

Bisociation Brainstorming is the basis for our visionary thinking approach. In this approach, we take future-focused knowledge we call Dynamic Knowledge, and see how two or more pieces of this dynamic knowledge intersect to uncover emerging opportunities or challenges. In this application of focused attention, we can create a pattern or a system where we can take this future-focused information, look at how they are interacting, and establish patterns of opportunity recognition. This will encourage a lot more sensational ideas.

I'll give you an example. One big trend is more people are using home computers. If you follow that trend, you might go into the computer manufacturing and sales business. But the computer business has very low profit margins. Another trend is more people are traveling. If you follow that trend and go into the travel agency business, you'll find a disrupted industry for retail travel agents. But if you put the two together—a social trend and a technology trend—you'll come up with an idea that has become very popular over the last seven or eight years of Internet-based travel agencies. Expedia and Orbitz together sold for over six billion dollars a few years ago. The point is, you would never have come up with that market opportunity unless you looked at the convergence of two dissimilar trends. This is what we call Bisociation Brainstorming, a patent-pending thinking process for "connecting the dots outside the box."

This is an example of analogical or non-logical thinking. It is also an example of convergent and divergent thinking. In this process, we converge trends and then come up with divergent ideas. It's a combination of some of the more popular patterns or thinking processes.

Wright

In your upcoming book, *Reinvent Your Business Model,* you talk about "Creative Disruption." What is this concept?

Rasheed

Creative Disruption is a metaphor for proactively looking for opportunities based on lessons in nature. We've used this metaphor from nature to construct a model for realizing sustainable innovation. A lot of things we have talked about are part of this model and it is supported by research in strategic management. It is centered on the idea of aligning people, environment, process, and technology for knowledge creation. This is a way that maximizes potential in an organization.

Creative Disruption is a nature-based metaphor we use to illustrate how we create a sustainable business ecosystem. The objective of this ecosystem is knowledge creation, the basis for innovation. As in nature, energy is absorbed from the root system of a plant in order to generate growth and sustain plant life. The radiation of the sun causes photosynthesis that stimulates growth and development. In business, knowledge creation is the essence of energy that needs to flow freely through people and the environment, using an efficient process supported by technology. Using examples from nature is a colorful way of looking at growth and development in your business and in your life.

We use metaphors from nature to label some of the innovation styles that we talked about earlier. For instance, the visionaries are the "radiators" that generate energy and enthusiasm for new ideas. People who exhibit the visionary-explorer profile are the "rain makers." These are the innovation champions who do not come up with ideas but do a great job bringing the ideas forth and marshalling resources. The explorer-experimenter profile represents the "harvester." In this profile, you will find the intrapraneurs are entrepreneurially-minded people who commercialize their new ideas within their existing organizations. They are the "mavericks" who push the boundaries of the organization to create something new and possibly outside the existing core competences.

Stakeholders who fit the experimenter profile are "landscapers." These are the project leaders who use their knowledge of subject matter and the environment to evaluate, organize, and plan the strategic initiatives.

The "pollinators" exhibit the characteristics of the experimenter-modifying profile. Pollinators are the thought leaders in the organization. They typically engage other departments with ideas and facilitate cross-fertilization of ideas and multi-functional activities, much like the behavior of bees that pollinate flowers in nature.

Finally, there those who are in the modifying profile. We call them the "cultivators." These are the stakeholders who do the research. They provide knowledge, scientific inquiry, and research-based validation of the innovation effort.

Wright

How will an innovation system contribute to achieving success?

Rasheed

If you consider what the potential value of the next big idea could be, leaving innovation to be random and serendipitous is not what industry leaders should do. We're suggesting that for an organization to be successful and for you to personally be successful, you need to have a systematic approach to innovation. That is what this ecosystem does, based on this Creative Disruption metaphor. We find that this innovation system will provide a sustainable approach that can be replicated throughout an organization. When you use this innovative thinking approach in your personal life, you become more creative. We find that this is what organizations need and it's what they value. Not only is it how you get the most out of your knowledge workers, but it also maximizes relationships with other stakeholders, your customers, and suppliers. This is a way to get them to be more involved in your value creation activities in a regular and organized manner.

We've all heard about focus groups with your customers and with your suppliers to get them to give input on how you can improve your products and services. Well, creating a system that allows them to do that more efficiently just makes a lot of sense. Having innovative thinking will maximize your human potential personally. If you pull together a diverse group of innovative thinkers with a replicable system of innovation, it makes it easier for them to collaborate and share information for innovation to occur.

For instance, in this ecosystem model, we use the example of the beehive. A beehive is actually the most efficient structure in nature and most people think it's a hexagon. It's actually ten-sided, and all the cells in that honeycomb fit together, with semipermeable boundaries. If you think about that in the context of an organization, in too many cases the only contact point between one department and another is the manager or the team leader. The generation of and actualizing new ideas often depend on the relationship between department heads. But the beehive example suggests that maybe you should have multifaceted contact points for sharing information so that this knowledge can transmit throughout the organization more effectively and efficiently. When people can share ideas you'll generate more effective processes and more effective ideas.

Wright

What are the five elements of a strategic ecosystem?

Rasheed

As we talked about earlier, the first one is knowledge. We must have not only good information and good data, but we also have to be able to share it and it has to be future focused. If you ask an entrepreneur or a businessperson whether he or she wants to "bet the farm" on old information or where the puck is going to be, the answer is obvious. But unfortunately, most of the attention in our organizations is focused on historical knowledge that is already written down or information that is in someone's head that we can't get out. Or worse yet, it's neither valued nor shared very effectively.

Using the ecosystem metaphor, knowledge is the energy of the ecosystem. If you don't have good knowledge and if it's not shared and it's not processed throughout the system, then you're not going to have innovation in the organization.

Secondly, you must also have innovative people. You need people who are creative, who have an innovative thinking process, who are willing to set aside their old mental models, their old assumptions, and paradigms, and process new information. If you do this consistently and regularly, you're going to have strong stakeholders who are empowered to create new ideas.

The third element is the environment. You've heard about having an innovative culture. If you look at the research on innovation, many managers talk about culture, but no one has established what that really means and how to make it happen consistently. Too often we talk about culture in terms of iconic CEOs like the Steve Jobs (Apple) and the Jack Welchs (GE) of the world. These are the iconic figures who radiate energy throughout their organizations and stimulate thought.

But not every organization has an iconic leader, so how do you create an innovative environment that processes information and empowers people on a consistent basis? One of the things we try to do is look at a company's environment in terms of its value network. You've heard of supply chains and value chains. Well, the value network is an extended version of that, in the sense that the value chain and the supply chain are organizationally based. An organizational perspective does not take into account all of your stakeholders such as your auditors, your product outsourcers, your labs, your investors, your suppliers, and your customers. How do you get external stakeholders involved in this innovation process and create a culture that perceives this information as truly shared and constructive? You Do it by understanding and using your value network.

Then you have to have a system or a process that makes the generation of ideas a consistent process. We've developed a seven-step process for harnessing the collective intelligence in your organization. This allows a free flow of information and is based on this very productive metaphor of nature. We have actually addressed some of the issues that are critical to the first five steps—assessment of your innovative styles, visualizing your environment, exploring dynamic knowledge, discovering opportunities, and innovating new ideas. The final two stages involve envisioning business models and scenarios and actualizing your ideas using strategic road maps and an innovation balanced scorecard.

Finally, you have to have technology. Collaborative technology enables an organization to innovate more effectively. We advise organizations on how to use software tools to archive their intellectual capital and make it accessible to stakeholders throughout the value network.

Wright

What are some of the typical market applications for your innovation system?

Rasheed

A typical application is a "Strategic Transformation" project— organizational change, and strategic planning projects. The objective is to strategically transform the organization and come up with change in a positive direction. We've helped organizations engage in strategic transformation brainstorming with our systems.

Another would be technology commercialization. A lot of the technology transfer organizations have a portfolio of great ideas that have come out of their university, sometimes funded by The National Science Foundation, The National Institution of Health, NASA, the Department of Defense, or private research and development. But this technology is sitting on a shelf because they don't have enough entrepreneurs who understand the technology or realize the opportunity for commercialization. We help organizations bring their scientists and their entrepreneurs together and brainstorm what some of those market opportunities are for some of this really great technology they have in their portfolio.

The third one is the new product development that we typically associate innovation with. This could be in the form of radical and breakthrough technology, or it could mean incremental innovation that makes the existing product lighter, faster, more through-put, or more bandwidth.

The fourth market we focus on is think tanks that are organized for strategic foresight. This group typically creates long-term economic development plans for the government or anticipates social and regulatory issues for and develops plans associated with these issues.

These are example of how stakeholders and leaders in a variety of industries and organizations can be proactive and search out opportunities rather than wait for the proverbial knock on the door that will probably never come.

Wright

What a great conversation. I can see how important this is and I really appreciate the opportunity to talk with you for this long. I really appreciate your answering all these questions for me.

Rasheed

I appreciate the opportunity, David. It's been a pleasure for me because I think innovation is critical to the success of our country as well as our global competitiveness.

Wright

Today we've been talking with Dr. Howard Rasheed. Dr. Rasheed is an innovation coach and trainer for empowering innovation champions in their search for competitiveness. He is an Associate Professor of Strategy and Innovation at the University of North Carolina in Wilmington, and he is the Founder of the Institute for Innovation.

Dr. Rasheed, thank you so much for being with us today on *Yes You Can!*

Rasheed

It has been my pleasure, David.

Howard Rasheed, PhD, writes and speaks on how to effectively accelerate innovation in organizations. Known internationally as the "Innovation Strategist," he leads a team of innovation consultants and trainers of techniques that empower innovative leaders in their search for competitiveness. He is an innovation coach and trainer for empowering innovation champions in their search for competitiveness. His upcoming book, *Reinvent Your Business Model: 7 Steps to Sustainable Innovation,* presents a simple but colorful metaphor of a strategic ecosystem for sustainable innovation. This science-based approach to innovation guides you to a renewable source of creative energy and transformational ideas. He has developed a proprietary system and software for innovating and ideation called "The Idea Accelerator." This science-based system has been used in applications for strategic transformation, think tanks, technology commercialization, and product development projects.

Dr. Rasheed is an Associate Professor of Strategy and Innovation at the University of North Carolina in Wilmington and Founder of the Institute for Innovation. He received his PhD in Global Strategic Management from Florida State University.

Howard Rasheed, PhD

3600 S. College Road, Suite 386
Wilmington, NC 28412
877-789-8899
hrasheed@idea-act.com

CHAPTER 6

CHALLENGE:
Adversity or Opportunity?

by Andréa Michaels

David Wright (Wright)

Today we're talking with Andréa Michaels. Andréa is the winner of more than thirty-four Special Event Gala Awards. She is also the first inductee into the Special Event Industry Hall of Fame, as well as the winner of two SITE Crystal Awards, an MPI Global Paragon Award, and many other industry recognitions. All of these are for impeccable and innovative strategy-based and targeted meetings and events. Prominent events include the opening of the Las Vegas Venetian Hotel, Lumiere Place in St. Louis, Town Square in Las Vegas, the opening of GM Place in Vancouver, and international road shows for the Hong Kong Tourist Bureau, Mercedes, BMW, as well as a variety of clients globally. Additionally, her seminars on creativity, the profitability of doing business, and Anatomy of an Event have earned her international kudos. In a few words, she sets the trends that others follow.

Andréa, welcome to *Yes You Can!*

Andréa Michaels (Michaels)

Thank you.

Wright

So what is your personal definition of adversity and how do you face it?

Michaels

I've been thinking about that question a lot. Is there really such a thing as adversity or is life a series of little jokes that are being played on us all the time? I think that every day we face a series of challenges and tests and it's all about how we meet them that determines if we see them as adversity or not. I don't necessarily see them as adversities; I see them more as opportunities. When something comes along that is unexpected, if you perceive it to be negative, it is adversity. If you see it as positive, it is an opportunity.

And how do I face "it"? Really, always head on, I try to figure out where I want to go, what the best way of getting there is, and then just look straight ahead. It's like driving a car—every once in a while you hit a detour, but that doesn't mean you turn around and go back. And it doesn't mean you stop and stay in one place. You just figure out what the best road is and what the destination is, and you keep heading toward that destination.

Wright

So what adversities have you faced in your personal life and how have you dealt with them?

Michaels

Well, considering that I'm limited to using only between four and six thousand words in this chapter, I'm really not going to list all of them, but they probably started from birth, before I could even determine what an adversity was. I was born in Croatia in a concentration camp and my mother and my grandparents and I escaped by a fishing boat across the Adriatic and went into hiding in Italy. During all those years we were being pursued and attacked.

After the liberation, my mother moved to the United States and I stayed with my grandparents. I would say that the first real adversity that I perceived was when I was sent for and arrived in the United States. I was six or seven years old and I had no clue who my mother was. The person who met me was a total stranger. I didn't speak a word of English and didn't have a clue who she was married to. Everything was new and had to be learned from scratch. The only person who had been my security, my grandmother, was now no longer in my life.

I think that at a very young age I learned immediately that one has to adapt. There was no choice. Later, at a certain point in my life, my parents (my mother had remarried) moved us to a community, which in the 1950s was very racist, for lack of a better word. I was just at that hormonal age when I was entering the world of being a teenager. We moved to a town called Burbank in Southern California, which was very Christian, very Mormon, very conservative, and very Republican. Here I had these two type A personalities—absolutely gorgeous parents—very European, very liberal, very Democratic. My mother always dressed me like some a young model out of Saks Fifth Avenue because that's what she knew from Europe. I was utterly out of place.

Added to that we were Jewish, so we were like the devils in that community. I mean everything that a black person might say they experienced thirty years ago, we experienced and then some, in a community where there were maybe eight to ten Jewish families. We were outcasts. My parents were treated like pariahs. My friends, who were Jewish, and I were the subjects of a lot of hostility, a lot of racism, so ultimately we had to figure out how to deal with it. I studied very hard. I wanted to be the best so I tried to make myself stand out in very positive ways that reflected well on me and my family. Those of us who were subjected to racism didn't adopt a posture of defense. I think that this is something I learned about adversity—you never have to come from a position of defense, you just have to rise above it. I was a very young girl when we learned those things.

Later relationships presented me personally with a lot of adversity. My marriages were not good choices. I have been married twice and had a long-term, live-in relationship as well. All three were with what I would call cads or men who didn't reflect good values, didn't treat me well, lied, cheated, or stole. I would call them immoral. Those were very personal adversities or challenges. I raised a child on my own. I returned to college to get a degree. I worked full-time to create a career path for myself. So juggling within a twenty-four-hour day what seemed like thirty-five hours of what I needed to do was also challenging.

All those things might be perceived as personal adversities. And again I just kept the end goal in sight and kept moving forward. Was it easy? No. But I don't believe that you are not in control of your own destiny. I had made bad choices and admitted that. But that didn't mean I couldn't move on.

Wright

What about business—what adversities have you faced in your business life?

Michaels

Well, let's see, I was involved in a bad business marriage you might say. It was a partnership that was very unbalanced. Toward the end, it became very adversarial in that I was bringing in the business and my partner was taking the credit. We didn't have the same goals, ideals, or ethical standards.

Eventually we had a very ugly parting of the ways. I thought I had taken the higher moral ground when I resigned from the partnership because I had consulted attorneys and accountants to find out what the law said I could and couldn't do, and I followed their advice to the letter. The day after I resigned from my partnership I was slapped with a forty-million-dollar lawsuit, even though I had followed all the rules. I had not taken anything out of the partnership—money, clients, anything. Yet I was being sued. I didn't want to get embroiled in a tattle-tale, he-said-she-said-they-said kind of situation, so I just tried to continue to do business in the most honorable way that I could. Eventually my ex-partner went bankrupt and I did very well.

I have been a victim of embezzlement and lost a lot of money in the process. I have had former employees steal money, steal clients, and leave under suspicious and unethical situations. I would call that business as usual. If you are financially prepared for whatever may come along, you don't get totally wiped out. And if you've developed good, honest relationships with your clients, most of them will choose to stay with you. Again, I think it's all in how you set yourself up so that when adversity or a challenge hits you in the face, it can't really harm you.

Wright

Do you see any differences between personal and business adversity?

Michaels

No. I really don't because anybody who tells you that when you're hit with business adversity not to take it personally is crazy. Of course it's personal. It's not impersonal if someone chooses not to work with you or if someone chooses to steal a client or steal your money. How can you look at the total picture and say it's not personal? It is.

Wright

So what are specific tools that you could share with our readers to overcome adversity in order to achieve success?

Michaels

First, carefully define "adversity" for yourself. Determine if you see the situation as something negative. Can you see this challenge as a warning sign, a detour? If so, then adversity can be a sign that says pay attention and figure out what you need to do to make things better.

I believe that when faced with adversity/challenge it's also a matter of staying calm, staying focused, not getting so stressed out that you can't look at your situations with a sense of reality, and organize yourself in such a way to overcome any situation that comes your way. I think that if you stay true and you stay honest, no matter what comes along, your path can be very direct. It's when you start convoluting your life with exceptions, with stresses, with little white lies, with excuses—mainly excuses—that you start not facing reality.

And adversity is a type of reality. It's like a sneeze. A sneeze tells you that you might be getting a cold, so maybe it's time to get proactive and make sure you don't get the cold—take vitamin C, sleep longer hours, don't go out and get a chill. Vaccinations are insurance against getting certain diseases, so get them. Otherwise, it's your own fault if you get sick.

Wright

As a business owner, how do you handle difficult adversarial situations and clients?

Michaels

With what I call well studied communications skills, very peaceful communication, and a whole lot of empathy. Very few people (let's talk about people first) I've encountered rarely intentionally want to be mean or hostile or even difficult. Most of them act those ways either out of discomfort or because they have a problem or there is a situation that has nothing to do with what you think is causing the problem. That's the time when I try to engage. So if I have a client who is being particularly difficult, I try to engage him or her in a conversation where I can learn what the real bothersome issue is, get past it, empathize with it, and find a solution. Once you present a solution instead of restating the problem over and over again or defending yourself against it, normally a client will calm down.

As far as challenging situations, I've experienced fires, hurricanes, tornadoes, and of course all of these lovely economic situations that are facing us now. The reality is that some things are just plain out of your control, so there is no point getting hysterical about them. Again, look at every situation calmly, meet with a team of people if you need to, figure out the best approach to come up with a solution, and act on it methodically and thoughtfully.

We had a situation a while back where we were doing a multimillion-dollar show in a park in Chicago and every single generator, including the back-up generators, blew up and we had no power for our show. There was a way of fixing it that would take a little time. We had the options of letting our client know what was happening, making excuses, or pretending that we knew exactly how to fix the problem, even if we didn't. There were just all kinds of possibilities. My choice was to go to my technical team and do a reality check—exactly what can we do, how long will it take, and is it a 100 percent reliable? Then to go to the client and say, here is our solution.

Clients and situations aren't difficult as long as you're not going to someone only with a complaint; that accomplishes nothing. Calm solutions, thoughtfulness, and honesty do.

Wright

Would you describe balance and how this affects facing diversity?

Michaels

I think if you achieve a state of balance—and I'd call that a common thoughtful approach to any situation, good or bad, adversarial or not—then it calms everyone around you. I've been reading the *Twilight* book series and one of the characters who has intrigued me is Jasper Hale, the one who has the gift of being able to bring people around him to a sense of peace and balance. I thought it would be wonderful if we could really do that. I think that a calm attitude is reassuring, both internally and externally. This requires looking at every situation and evaluating what it really means in the larger scheme of things; this can be very calming.

Some people get hysterical over little things. In my profession, that might be an actor or musician who is three minutes late arriving at a job. My attitude is, does that really matter? It's not as good as being on time, but will it so drastically affect everything? Potentially, the chaos that would ensue if you got overly upset affects everything else and then it produces a trickle-down effect from there. Prioritize what's important and what's not. Then just get rid of what's not important and don't even think about it anymore. Just concentrate on the things that are most important and how to achieve them. To me, that's balance.

Wright

So what personally motivates you in order to achieve this balance?

Michaels

I want calm and peace in my life. I grew up with very volatile parents and I surrounded myself with very volatile relationships. I think I have a right to demand for myself—and to pass on to others—peace and calm and well-being. Without that, nothing else is really very good. Let yourself feel great about things that are good. Eliminate and don't even give thought to the things that are bad because it doesn't get you anywhere—you will not gain anything from dwelling on negative things. I'm all about what you want to get out of life and what you gain from any given situation.

It all stems from understanding yourself and others. I've learned that if you don't understand something, ask a question, check things out, and don't make assumptions. Assumptions are a killer. You think you know what someone else means, you think you know what others are thinking, but how often are you wrong? Take the time to check things out. That's really important.

Wright

So if you could place yourself in the mindset of our readers, what questions do you suppose they might have and how would you address them?

Michaels

Most people will ask me why I don't ever get stressed out. If they're addressing that question to me personally, I would probably engage them in my life story. The reality is that if you have been born to two Holocaust survivors who lived in concentration camps and spent their youth running from Nazis, you would find it very hard to convince me that some of the little things that stress other people out are very important. If someone doesn't die from it, doesn't get sick before my eyes, and if it isn't life-threatening, I just don't think it counts that much.

I think most people want to know how to handle stress because most people get very stressed out. How do you protect yourself from adversity? I don't think you can protect yourself if your mindset perceives it as adversity. So once again, it's all about how you communicate with yourself. When something presents itself as a roadblock, does life or your journey stop? If you know your destination—a job, an education, a relationship—then you always know what you need to do to get there.

I think people need to prepare themselves. They can't just always experience happenstance. Yes, you can take it as it comes, but with a plan in mind so that you know if you encounter an obstacle what you can do about it. It's like little kids with video games—things are constantly flying at them that they have to shoot at. Then somebody pops out of some box somewhere and it's a good guy. You don't want to shoot the good guy. So you need to adapt so that when the unexpected does happen you don't lose the game.

Wright

It seems to me that you might have changed over time. Has that change been difficult?

Michaels

I think the major change I have made was to have a more defined sense of self, which has helped me deal with challenges better. Up until a few years ago, my life was so outer directed. I felt a need to please everyone at all costs, no matter what it did to me personally. I don't think anybody benefited from that. I think that as I've grown as an individual, I have realized this. I have to believe that I can be appreciated for who I am and not what I do. It has given me a better perspective; I can make a stand knowing what's right and what's wrong and stick to it without going along with what someone else might expect, even if it's wrong for me. I think that's been the major change.

Wright

Do you think that's confidence?

Michaels

Self-assuredness and confidence? I don't know—are they the same?

Wright

Sounds like it to me. It sounds as though you've been able to change for the better and it hasn't been as hard as you might have thought.

Michaels

No, it hasn't and it comes from listening and asking—what I was talking about before. Check things out and don't make assumptions. When you're insecure, you're always worrying if someone is unhappy with you or doesn't like what you're doing. You constantly think you have to change and make others happy. It's almost desperation. I don't feel that sense of desperation anymore.

Interestingly, a conversation with my son (who is turning forty this year) led me to something that taught me lot in business as well as personal relationships. He and I were occasionally argumentative with each other, yet we love each other dearly and have a great relationship. But every once in a while, the working and personal relationship got testy. I have a beautiful, wonderful daughter-in-law and two gorgeous grandchildren. I think that the most important part of my life is my family, so I really want to make the relationship with my son as good as it can be.

One day I asked him, "If you or your wife would want any one thing about our relationship to change, is there anything I personally could do to make it better?"

"Yes," he replied, "you can stop trying to fix everything for everybody. Sometimes when I talk to you about a problem I don't want you to fix it. You're my mother; I just want to talk to you and I want you to hear me."

I thought about that, because if someone says, "I have a problem," I'll jump right in to try to fix it.

After my talk with my son, now when he comes to me and says, "Can we talk?" my first question is, "Is this personal?" My second question is, "Do you want me just to listen, or are you asking me for advice or a solution?"

When we identified that problem, our conversations became so much easier and so much more rewarding for both of us.

This experience taught me about clients, also. Ask the question. If people tell you they've got a problem with your way of working, you don't have to assume it's the kiss of death. It's an opportunity to listen and absorb the clues. Maybe it will require a solution and at other times it will just require empathy because it may have nothing to do with you at all. It may be what your client's boss has said to him or her earlier that day.

Wright

Finally, when do you simply walk away and not deal with adversity at all?

Michaels

When it's wrong for you and when you know it's wrong for you, when there is no possible way to fix what is happening, and you know you can't make someone happy. Take a look at the clients who always say, "Can you do if for less?" You so badly want to make them happy, but you're going to lose money, so walk away. If you have offered every solution that you know to be right, and the other person can't accept it, walk away. Do not do what you know to be wrong just to please someone else. When people want refunds for things you know they shouldn't get refunds for, and they say things to you like, "Well, if you want to work for us ever again, you will do thus and so," never give that refund or discount because you'll never see them again anyway. Once people know they can abuse you, they'll abuse you forever.

So don't let people take advantage of you. Stand up for your rights. Be confident. If you know something is right and if you know something is good for you, that's a good enough reason to stick to it. You don't have to not treat people well. There are just certain things that are important in life and you have to commit to your sense of self- worth and stay with it.

Wright

Well, what a great conversation. The next time I need any advice, I'll call you and I'll tell you whether I want you to listen.

Michaels

I look forward to it. And I'll listen.

Wright

Oh my, now I know why you are so successful. I really appreciate all this time you've taken with me today to talk about this important subject.

Michaels

I thank you for your time and I'm very appreciative of the questions and how well you listened to me.

Wright

Today we've been talking with Andréa Michaels. Andréa is the winner of more than thirty-four Special Event Gala Awards and the first inductee into the Special Event Industry Hall of Fame. She is also winner of two SITE Crystal Awards and the MPI Global Paragon Award. I think her forté might be her seminars on creativity, the profitability of doing business, and the Anatomy of an Event. These have certainly gained her many kudos throughout the years. The next time she has one I think I might go.

Andréa, thank you so much for being with us today on *Yes You Can!*

Michaels

My pleasure.

Andréa is the winner of more than thirty-four Special Event Gala Awards, the first inductee into the Special Event Industry Hall of Fame as well as a winner of two SITE Crystal Awards, an MPI Global Paragon Award, two EIBTM (international) awards, and a slew of other recognitions. She is also among the one hundred largest woman-owned businesses in Los Angeles. All accolades are for impeccable and innovative meetings and events. Prominent events include the openings of Las Vegas' Venetian Hotel, Lumiere Place in St. Louis, Town Square in Las Vegas, GM Place in Vancouver, B.C., and international road shows for Mercedes, Hong Kong Tourist Board, and many others of distinction.

Her seminars on Creativity, The Profitability of Doing Business, and Anatomy of an Event have earned her inéternational kudos. The summation? She sets the trends that others follow. Her autobiographical book, *Reflections of a Successful Wallflower, Lessons in Life, Lessons in Business,* was published in March 2010.

Andréa Michaels

Extraordinary Events

818-783-6112

amichaels@extraordinaryevents.net

CHAPTER 7

Say *Yes* to Personal Branding

by Marva L. Goldsmith, AICI, CIP

David Wright (Wright)

Today we're talking with Marva Goldsmith. She has built her reputation on the delivery of unique programs addressing change, image, and personal brand management through workshops, coaching, and her consulting services. An electrical engineer with more than twenty-five years of business and leadership experience, Marva returned to school at the age of forty-one to receive a master's degree in Public Administration from Harvard University with a concentration in Leadership. She then studied image management with DominiQue IsbecQue International, the London Image Institute, and the Image Resource Group. She has earned the designation of Certified Image Professional, which is held by less than one hundred and fifty image consultants in the entire United States, from the Association of Image Consultants International. She obtained additional leadership training through The Center for Creative Leadership and Georgetown University's Leadership Coaching Program.

Marva is the author of six workbooks including Branding Yourself After Age 50, Creating Brand Strategy for Your life, Branding You, Inc., and Marketing Yourself for the Future.

Marva Goldsmith, welcome to *Yes You Can!*

Marva Goldsmith (Goldsmith)

Thank you, David. It's a pleasure to be here.

Wright

So why should I care about personal branding?

Goldsmith

Today, it is especially important to stand out in this very competitive career and business marketplace. According to *American Demographics* magazine, seven Baby Boomers will turn fifty every minute in the United States from now until 2014. There are more than sixteen million Americans fifty-five and older who are either working or seeking work.

A person who establishes an intentional personal brand attracts more business or job opportunities than a person who presents himself or herself as an indistinguishable product. *What do I mean by that?* When you think about a product as an example, you might think of chicken, however, a brand is Kentucky Fried Chicken, or Popeye's. The product—chicken—is indistinguishable and is generally sold based on price. If you purchase chicken at your local grocery, you will likely purchase based on price and expiration date. It does not matter what brand is being sold. But, both KFC and Popeye brands are *distinct* in the marketplace. You expect a certain taste and quality of service. Similarly, in a career or business environment, products don't stand out, they're not distinguishable. By creating yourself as a brand, you begin to communicate your distinguishing attributes— your Unique Selling Proposition (USP)—to the marketplace. You understand what makes you different and special and more importantly, you are able to articulate that to your target market—employers, customers, and existing clients.

Your USP is the implicit promise that you are providing to your clients, prospects, or potential employers in exchange for doing business with you or hiring or promoting you. A few well known examples of commercial products that offer unique selling propositions are: Domino's Pizza: "Fresh, hot pizza delivered to your door in 30 minutes or less—or it's free" and FedEx: "When your package absolutely, positively has to get there overnight." Implicit in these examples are the targets' pain points and the promises made to solve the targets' challenges.

Similarly, your USP is a distinct idea that distinguishes you and your business from every other competitor. It is developed for each target market. It answers the question of "What value can you provide to your target that will help solve a problem, increase market share, or improve business?"

Wright

So what does personal branding mean exactly?

Goldsmith

Personal branding is simply a way to identify what makes you different and special. It then communicates these characteristics in a way that your marketplace can distinguish you from all the other products on the shelf. These distinguishing attributes then guide your career and business decisions.

Wright

We often hear the term "personal branding" in relation to social media. Does one have to have an online presence and how does that online presence in social media affect one's personal brand?

Goldsmith

Remember the beginning of the computer revolution? The naysayers said, "No one is going to buy a computer for his or her home." According to a 2005 study by Seagate Corporation, 76 percent of adults own a personal computer. Now we're at a point where everyone who is serious about branding themselves should have an online presence. If people are considering your small business to work for them, they'll go to the Internet and Google your name and your company name. If you are not on the 'Net, they will be forced to form an opinion based on a lack of information. Having no Web site suggests that either you haven't been in business very long or you haven't done a lot of work. These days, if someone really wants to understand who you are in the marketplace, the first thing he or she does is go online. This concept does not escape professionals who are seeking employment.

The next step of building an online presence is to participate in other online communities to add value to the discussion in which you're branding yourself. By that, I mean blogging or answering a question on someone else's blog. For example, if you want to increase your credibility in a certain industry, you might start a blog and talk about various aspects of that business to demonstrate your expertise—not selling your services, but simply adding value to the conversation. You can do that as well on some of the social media sites like LinkedIn or Biznik. There are many social networking sites that will allow you to establish your online presence. As you provide value and accurate information (very important), you will become associated with that industry and eventually you will be branded as an expert.

If blogging scares you or seems like too big a time commitment, you can begin by joining a group associated with your industry or field of work on LinkedIn. You will notice people posting questions, or you can start a discussion related to a topic in your field of expertise. Then, by answering questions from other people, adding information to their posts, or posting discussions about your field of expertise, you can begin to craft an understanding in this marketplace of who you are, what you know, and how you add value to the conversation.

Wright

This social media thing is just really sweeping the country. If you don't do it, what is the downside? What's going to happen to you?

Goldsmith

Well, it's like everything else. If you're not present, you are allowing other people to make some of the decisions about who you are in the marketplace. Famed management guru Peter Drucker said it best, "Branding, by its very nature, is not optional. If you do not position yourself in people's minds, they will do it for you." If you have no presence in the marketplace the only decision your target market can make is that you're not active, and you are not a part of the critical mass of thinking about this particular subject. So if you're not present, then how can you really profess to be an expert in that field? As I work with Baby Boomers who are reinventing themselves, either by default or design, I urge them to get engaged in the social media revolution.

Wright

I can see that. So how is personal branding similar to branding a commercial product?

Goldsmith

I love to use ketchup as an example of something that is understood by most people. It has the same ingredients, no matter what brand you pick up. You have tomatoes, spices, and some sort of sugar. As such, ketchup could be considered to be an indistinguishable product. However, the number one brand in the ketchup industry is Heinz Ketchup. How did the company distinguish itself from all the other brands of ketchup on the shelf? Heinz identified what made its product different and special. The company marketed its product as the thicker, richer ketchup.

You may remember a campaign of dueling ketchup bottles. Heinz, of course, was the "slowest ketchup in the West." This was followed by commercials with Carole King singing *Anticipation*. Heinz created the perception of being the slower, thicker, richer ketchup. When people want ketchup that is going to stick on the French fry, they're going to reach for Heinz Ketchup. The question becomes, is Heinz really the slowest, richest, thickest ketchup on the shelf? Maybe, and maybe not, but more than 40 percent of the market perceives that it is and those buyers choose Heinz. That is an excellent example of branding and how it can work for you and help you define yourself relative to others with the same product or service.

As we develop our personal brands, we should remember the Heinz example. First, you have to understand the product, and question what makes it different and special. Once you understand the product—*you*— you can begin to create that perception of uniqueness within your business or career.

As an example, there are other people, of course, in the image industry who create workshops, coach, and consult on personal branding. I have created a niche as a personal branding expert who works with mid-career professionals. I am the image consultant and brand coach who will help Baby Boomers successfully brand themselves to compete for new jobs, new business, and higher visibility. To that end, I wrote a book called *Branding Yourself After Age 50*. I have spoken at forums for mid-career professionals such as the AARP Life@50+ National Conference, written articles for online magazines that specifically target Baby Boomers, like *More Magazine* (www.more.com), and I also have a blog, a fan page on Facebook, and a group on LinkedIn named after the book.

The objective is to continuously identify ways to participate in the conversation about personal branding for people who are at the midlife stage and must reinvent themselves, their business, or their career. My goal is to be established in a narrower field with distinctive expertise. Now, that does not suggest that I do not work in other markets, but when people are looking for a branding expert who focuses on midlife reinventions, I want them to reach for Marva Goldsmith.

In this particular career environment, with the economy being what it is, there are so many people who are at the mid part of their career, in midlife, going about their own business and now are faced with either the possibility of being laid off, have already been laid off, or have been offered a buy-out package. They want to continue working but just don't know what to do next. Some of these people have been in their industry for, ten, fifteen, or twenty years, and have not been in the career marketplace. Consequently, they are uncertain as to how to procure new work or a new position. In this marketplace, old tactics are irrelevant. You have to brand the product!

You have to ask yourself, "What is my sweet spot? Where do my experiences, my skills, and my value collide with the needs of my target market?"

Wright

So how do I enhance my personal brand? Are there steps that I can follow?

Goldsmith

Yes. There are three steps you should consider. First and foremost, you must establish yourself as a leader in something. Let's say you're working in a human resource field where there are lots of human resource strategists. It could be said that there are lots of indistinguishable products on the shelf, though you have a skill set that stands out. You might be a fantastic organizer. You need to create the perception of being the most organized person within your group of HR strategists. Then, people within your company or agency will start to recognize you as the "go to" person for organization. You will have defined how you want to be perceived and how you distinguish yourself from all of the other products on the shelf.

The second step is to get visibility for that role. Continuing with the HR example, if you are the most organized person in the HR group and you want to be known for that skill, you will have to create or find opportunities in which you can demonstrate that leadership role. You might volunteer to facilitate staff meetings or retreats. By organizing the meeting, creating the agenda, and making sure the meeting runs smoothly, you become recognized for your organizational skills.

The third area is consistency. You must remain consistent. If your leadership role within your HR team is based around organization skills and your desk is a disorganized mess, it is not consistent with the image you are trying to establish. You must be consistent in your approach to the marketplace as well. You cannot organize one great event and expect to be considered an expert. Your skills must be demonstrated continuously if you are to become a leader in the field. It is very important to understand these three aspects of creating brand strategy. Establish a leadership role. Obtain visibility for the role. Consistently deliver on your brand promise.

Remember former NBA star Dennis Rodman? He is a perfect example of ingenious and absolutely unique personal branding. Throughout the years he transformed himself, developing the Dennis Rodman brand into what his NBA.com bio calls "one of the most recognized athletes in the world." Rodman was a leader in his marketplace, the National Basketball Association. He would stop at nothing to get the ball. He was arguably one of the best rebounders in the history of the game and has five championship rings to back up his claim.

What Rodman did brilliantly, and in a most unconventional way, was gain visibility. He started by changing his appearance both on and off the court. He was constantly altering his hair color, flashing multiple tattoos, and displaying numerous body piercings. His metamorphosis from Dennis Rodman of the Detroit Pistons to Dennis Rodman of the Chicago Bulls was headline news on both the sports and entertainment pages. He became a celebrity and began to appear on talk shows. This was not just because he was a fierce rebounder. Talk show hosts could count on his outrageous behavior and eccentric appearance. Being extreme is what made him different, notable, and very *special*.

Ultimately, successful branding will lead to a purchase or a decision. It certainly did in Rodman's case. He made movies, appeared on reality television shows, and wrote two bestselling books. My favorite demonstration of his brand strength is the commercial he made for milk producers. Wearing a milk mustache, and with his buff chest bared, Rodman sent a message without saying a word. Why would producers of such a wholesome product as milk hire Dennis Rodman?

Wright

It would be a product endorsement, and I would also think that even though he is strange and unique, like everybody else, he needs milk.

Goldsmith

Yes, the message is clear: even bad boys drink milk. The milk producers hired Rodman because his brand coincided with the message they were trying to deliver. So when you walk into a room, when your name is mentioned, ideally something should immediately come to mind for people about who you are and what you represent.

David, when you walk into a room, when people see you, they automatically think about speakers. You have created visibility for your expertise—developing and promoting quality speakers—in a variety of different ways. You have trained speakers, established a speakers' network, met planners who probably rely on you to deliver a certain caliber of speaker, and you are most likely consistent in your approach to the market. Indeed, publishing this book and others like it is a part of that strategy. Utilizing these branding strategies will allow you to get the results that you are ultimately looking for. That is the whole purpose of personal branding.

Wright

So for people who are unemployed or underemployed how can personal branding help them?

Goldsmith

Personal branding has changed the way job hunters approach the market. Some people will go to an interview and use it as the embodiment of their resume. They write a resume, identify some targets, and secure an interview because of one great resume, but that's where it stops. The difference between a job hunter and a person who is intentional about their personal brand is that one is an undistinguishable product with a resume and the other is a brand with a marketing plan. By recognizing themselves as a brand, they understand who they should target and what their unique selling proposition with respect to each target is. In other words, they know what makes them compelling, what the target needs, and how to fulfill those needs. The personal brander likely has a blog or has volunteered in an area that provides an opportunity to demonstrate his or her value-added skills.

Many job hunters believe they must sell themselves. They present an image. This is what I do, this is my experience, and this is who I am. A job hunter with a personal brand orientation is going to ask as many questions of the interviewer as the interviewer asks of him or her. These job hunters are going to take on the role of consultants to learn about the companies' pain points and needs. Then, personal branders will make the connection between what the target needs and their distinguishing attributes. It is a very different orientation.

Job hunters must consider the question of visibility. Personal branders will position themselves by networking within their target industries. They will join an industry-specific association, become an active participant in the association, and then continuously demonstrate the value they provide to this industry. Personal branders will consistently get visibility for their leadership role because they have found a way to add value to an organization or an industry.

At the beginning of our conversation I talked about how products are sold. Indistinguishable products are consumed whereas brands are sought after, selected, and then purchased. People have to think about how they fit in the marketplace and about how they present themselves. They must develop themselves as a brand in order to succeed.

Wright

So would you tell our readers and our listeners what results you or your clients have experienced from developing a personal branding strategy?

Goldsmith

One of my favorite stories is about my first personal branding client. This gentleman called me because he was fearful of being fired from his teaching job. We started by conducting a short 360 degree assessment to understand how he was perceived in the marketplace. I asked him a series of questions including what distinguished him from others in his field. I then presented the same set of questions to a group of clients, managers, colleagues, and peers he selected. We understood not only how he distinguished himself, but what others counted on him to deliver: his brand promise.

We packaged the brand (clothing) in a way that was consistent with the vision he had for himself. After we packaged him well, and he understood the difference between his self-perception and how others perceived him, we worked to close that gap. About a month later, he informed me that not only had he retained his old job but he was being considered to become the principal at another school, and he eventually was hired.

His confidence had improved tremendously and he focused on the strengths that others perceived about who he was in the marketplace.

Wright

Well, what an interesting conversation. Branding is something that has always fascinated me.

Goldsmith

It's so important for people to be intentional about the branding process, because everybody has a brand. Your brand is at work twenty-four hours a day. The difference is that most people allow their brands to be created accidentally, without their vision in mind. It is very important to develop a vision and then create a brand strategy that is in alignment with your vision. Your target audience can expect that you will deliver something—a product, a service, a solution, a change—and that you will do so in a certain predictable manner.

Wright

That's a great distinction.

Marva, I really do appreciate all the time you've taken with me this morning to talk about branding and personal branding, and making it clear for a lot of us. I've learned a lot here today and I'm sure this chapter is really going to be helpful to our readers.

Goldsmith

Well, thank you so much. I appreciate this opportunity.

Wright

Today we've been talking with Marva Goldsmith. Marva delivers unique programs addressing change, image, and personal brand management through her workshops, coaching, and consulting services. She is the author of six workbooks including *Branding Yourself After Age 50, Creating Brand Strategy for Your Life,* and *Branding You, Inc.*

Marva, thank you so much for being with us today on *Yes You Can!*

Goldsmith

Thank you, David

Marva knows the transformation process intimately because she has lived it. She began her career as an electrical engineer and has held positions that include federal lobbyist, call center manager, and human resources strategist. At the age of forty-two, she obtained a master's degree in Public Administration with a concentration in Leadership from Harvard University. Marva then studied image management with Dominique Isbecque International, the London Image Institute, and the Image Resource Group. She received additional leadership training through the Center for Creative Leadership and Georgetown University's Leadership Coaching Program.

Certified Image Professional. Marva is one of fewer than one hundred and fifty consultants in the United States to be designated by the Association of Image Consultants International (AICI) as a Certified Image Professional.

Professional Speaker and Author. Marva has worked with clients as diverse as Fortune 500 companies and incarcerated youth, always spreading the good news about image and personal branding. Since 2005, Marva has published six workbooks, including *Branding Yourself After Age 50, Creating Brand Strategy for Your Life,* and *Marketing Yourself for the Future.* She has spoken at national and regional conferences, including the 2009 National AARP and Society of Human Resource Management (SHRM) Conferences, 2005 and 2003 National Training Officer's Conference, 2004 National Blacks in Government Conference, and Regional SHRM Conferences (2009–New Hampshire, 2008–New York, 2006–New Jersey).

Marva L. Goldsmith

4423 Lehigh Street, #232
College Park, MD 20740
301.474.8808
marva@marvagoldsmith.com
www.marvagoldsmith.com
www.branding50.com

CHAPTER 8

Flying on the Wings of Faith

by Amy Hymes, PhD

THE INTERVIEW

David Wright (Wright)

Today we are fortunate to have Dr. Amy Hymes as a contributing author for our discussions on achieving success and reaching your potential. Dr. Hymes speaks from her real world experiences as a psychologist, an international trainer, success-maker coach, entrepreneur, corporate advisor to CEOs and business executives, and president/CEO of a highly successful management consulting and training company. These experiences are backed up with academic discipline and the rigor of a doctorate in the area of psychology.

Dr. Hymes is a natural health practitioner and a student of human potential. She has a passion for helping others succeed that stems from her struggles faced in dealing with losing her mother at the age of nineteen and having to overcome her own self-limiting beliefs.

Today, Dr. Hymes currently practices organizational psychology and successfully supports individuals with making positive behavior change, and assists organizations with building a strong human capital team. She consults, trains, and helps to develop executives, managers, and key employees around the globe. She is known for her inspiring speeches and her ability to capture her audiences. Dr. Hymes specializes in helping individuals change their mindsets and behavior to live the life they truly desire.

Dr. Hymes, welcome to *Yes You Can!*

Amy Hymes (Hymes)

Thank you, David. I'm truly honored to be a part of this project.

Wright

So tell me, what do you contribute your success to?

Hymes

First and foremost, I contribute my success to my strong belief and unwavering faith in God!

Secondly, whenever I reflect back on how I got to where I am today, it always requires me to go all the way back to the very beginning of my life. You see, I grew up in very humble beginnings. I was born and raised in a small rural area of Johns Island, South Carolina, and I did not have access to many millionaires or super successful people to look up to. My family did not have much and were not career-oriented or educated people. They were not forward thinking people, and did not have a success plan for me to follow. My parents performed as their parents did. Their sole purpose in life was to focus on getting food on the table, keeping a roof over our heads, and keeping us clothed. You see, they did not have "disposable income" for us to explore development programs, participate in training seminars, or partake in extravagant outings. But what they did have and offered us was priceless. We had two hard-working parents with lots of love for each other and lots of love, discipline, and structure for us kids.

Fortunately for me, my mother instilled in me a strong sense of persistence. She always said, "Nothing will come easy in life; you must be persistent in whatever you do." I have kept those words in my mind throughout my life. So for that, I will forever be indebted to my loving parents, James and Angelena.

Also, I always believed deep down inside that I would get out of that environment and "break the mold" for my family. As far back as I can remember, I can recall being a big dreamer and having a big dream for myself; I always had a plan to do big things.

Now, there were also several other major factors that contributed to my success. Another that comes to mind is my passion for studying and researching successful people. Believe it or not, I always went to the library and checked out books on the thinking of extremely successful people and individuals who taught about wealth and success strategies. I was always a big reader of self-help books, wealth publications, and extravagant living magazines. I always told myself that I needed to prepare to live a successful lifestyle. Although I did not have riches when growing up, in my mind I always believed that I needed to "prepare" myself for how the rich lived so that I would be ready to step into those shoes when the opportunity presented itself. Accordingly, I always visualized what it would be like to live a prosperous life. Of course, what I did not know then was that I was mentally preparing for the life I live today. So I guess I could not have gotten to where I am today without first learning how to visualize what I desired and following a specific success plan. This is what I learned from self-improvement books and learning how to follow in the footsteps of other highly successful people who had achieved the success that I desired.

From reading and absorbing success and personal development materials, I developed mentoring relationships with some of the greatest people who ever lived. Now, of course, some of these people I have never actually met, and others lived long before my time, but their words were monumental to my development. Individuals like Jim Rohn, Napoleon Hill, Joseph Murphy, James Allen, Wallace D. Wattles, Norman Vincent Peele, Charles Haanel, and many others became my success teachers and guides. Their theories and philosophies will remain in my heart and mind for decades to come.

The Bible was also another great book that helped in my growth and advancement. The Bible is one of those books that many people sometimes forget about. But I still can evoke the scriptures in the books of Proverbs and Hebrews that expanded my mind. I learned about three concepts from the Bible that have become the cornerstone of my success: gain wisdom, knowledge, and faith.

Finally, another belief that was vital to my success was developing the correct mindset. For me, I decided a long time ago that I was going to be very successful, so I had to learn how to develop a success mentality and surround myself with other people who were on a journey to greatness. This meant that I had to concentrate my efforts on learning how the mind works, gaining specialized knowledge, learning how to become an entrepreneur, and developing products and services that would truly help others grow and develop. I had to learn how to become abundantly successful while remaining grounded and humble.

I started to model my behavior and practices after other extremely successful people like Ms. Oprah Winfrey. Since she was a business owner, I knew I had to own businesses. Since she started out in radio, I knew I had to become a radio talk show personality. Since she was a television talk show hostess, I knew I had to develop an informative and inspiring television talk show. It was just as simple as that—I followed a plan. These things did not happen overnight; however, the concepts were always in my success plan.

In line with these plans, something that always resonates in my mind is a saying by my mentor, Jim Rohn. He said, "In life we put the valuable things on the top shelf and in order to reach them we have to stand on the books that we read." So I say to anyone out there who has a big dream of becoming successful: you can do it, too; just start out by developing your plan. Even if you have nothing now, start by reading books and developing a success mindset. Then, continue on to study the methods of other successful people who have done what you want to attain. From there, move on to surrounding yourself with positive-minded people. You see, I am not successful because of family heritage or being brought up in a successful environment. Rather, I am a product of discipline, focus, vision, and taking effective action toward my success plan. I never allowed my situation or upbringing to define who I was or where I was going in life.

I believe I can contribute my success to five major factors:

1. Having unwavering faith in God,
2. Inspiration from what I did not have growing up and not wanting the complacency lifestyle that I saw growing up,
3. Developing a prosperous mindset and following a success model,
4. Persistence and taking effective action,
5. Developing a business model that produces products and services that truly help others to grow and develop.

Wright

How did you come to the decision to become an entrepreneur and a psychologist?

Hymes

You know, that question comes up quite a bit and the answer is rather simple. For me, I needed to be 100 percent in control of my destiny, so that is why I became an entrepreneur and business owner. I became a psychologist because I was fascinated by how the mind works and I wanted to know how I could help others grow, change, and develop. More importantly, I realized a long time ago that when other people are in control of your future, they do not always take you where you want to go. Because I knew where I wanted to go in life, I realized that I just needed people to help me understand how to get there.

In researching my path to success, I recognized that I could combine two loves—business and psychology—into something great. Actually, I can recall listening to a training CD from personal development expert, Zig Ziegler. He said, "You can have everything in life you want if you will just help enough other people get what they want." That is certainly the viewpoint I adopted and modeled my business after. I strive to educate, develop, and motivate individuals to reach their peak potential. In doing that, I utilize all of my God-given gifts and talents to help others grow! When you combine psychology and business, you end up with services like the ones we provide at Hymes & Associates Consulting, and topics like the ones we discuss on the *Development Connection* radio show.

In my business, we offer all psychology-based services to help individuals with their personal development endeavors, professional career advancement, and entrepreneurial mastery skills. Our services include: leadership training classes, self-improvement seminars, one-on-one coaching, management training, human capital management consulting, and organization development initiatives to help organizations grow their people and increase revenue, while at the same time helping individuals to become better.

Wright

In your opinion, what do you believe it takes to become abundantly successful?

Hymes

There are several things that one can do to become successful in life. First and foremost, you must form a clear picture of where you want to go in life and what you want to accomplish. From there you must develop a plan of action. Six strategies that immediately come to mind are the following:

1. *Train Your Mind for Success*—Our brain can be changed or trained to meet all of our life dreams. The mind is one of the most powerful tools that we have at our disposal. To train your mind for success, you must get your conscious and subconscious mind working together. It is your mind (your thinking) that determines your success. This is why it is so important for us to develop the ability to dream big!

   There are two parts of the brain that determine success or failure in life: the conscious and subconscious mind. The conscious part of the brain thinks and reasons for us. It can accept or reject any idea or concept that it wants. Therefore, it will decide how much success you will achieve in life tomorrow by the thoughts you choose to think today. All of your thoughts that you are thinking right now eventually will determine the results in your destination tomorrow. Your mind works in *pictures* and your thoughts *become things*. This is why we must learn how to control our thoughts and form a strong desire and belief system that we will succeed.

   The subconscious mind, on the other hand, is more powerful than the conscious mind because it does not have limits. The subconscious mind wants to keep us safe; therefore, it will fight against us making positive changes in our lives. It will magnify whatever you impress upon it. Every thought your conscious mind chooses to believe, the subconscious mind must accept. It has no ability to reject or form a thought. As we accept a thought, it is impressed upon our subconscious mind and then we literally become what we think about. By law, it expresses itself through us—in *feelings and actions*. Any thought that you consciously choose to think about over and over again will become fixed in this part of your mind.

   Our fixed ideas are commonly referred to as our habits and it is our habits that move our bodies into action. We may have a really strong desire to attain something, but as long as our subconscious mind is not aligned with our conscious mind, nothing will ever happen to manifest the desire.

So in other words, we have to change our thinking if we want to attain our desired goals. This is important to understand because we actually respond to what we observe with a positive or negative feeling, which then gives off a vibration to the Universe that will attract to us what we constantly think about. The *actions* that we take today will determine our results tomorrow, which will direct our success. Accordingly, it becomes vitally important that we learn to concentrate on sending out only positive vibrations and feelings.

Thoughts + Feelings + Actions = *Results*

In order to reach the results that we truly desire, we must control our thoughts and then release our vibrations and feelings to the Universe and allow it to manifest into what we truly desire.

It is also very important to recognize that our mind can actually hold us captive. Because of conditioning, our beliefs can become set, which can deprive us of attempting to change our behavior.

2. *Eliminate Negative Thinking*—Know that you are only limited by your own thoughts! Scientists, doctors, and the medical community can finally prove that there is scientific data on the remarkable healing powers of positive thinking. Experts say that there is clearly a connection between what you think and believe and how the body works.

Positive thinking and positive beliefs actually lead to a healthier and longer life. The power of positive thinking can and will change your life, but first you must get rid of your negative thoughts and change your belief system. Those who have a negative attitude or who focus on negative thoughts are more likely to have major setbacks in life and suffer detrimental effects on their health and on their bodies. Research has now confirmed that the mind, the brain, and the body's defense system actually communicate and talk with each other by way of special pathways and chemicals called neurotransmitters and hormones.

There is strong evidence to show that how we think, what we believe, and how we see the world all combine to shape our destiny and have a *dramatic* impact on our health. So we must stop the negative talk and negative thinking.

Instead, begin to create and maintain a positive attitude. Train your mind to focus on positive aspects of your life and create positive beliefs that will not only allow you to succeed, but will also make you feel better. Decide today that you will only focus on the positive aspects of things. If something does not add value, prosper you, or build you up, then you should not spend frivolous time discussing or concentrating on that particular thought or action. *Do not allow others to make you a negative person!*

3. *Create a Positive Belief System*—Our beliefs are concepts we have accepted from our past; therefore, we can eliminate or substitute them just as easily. Your belief system will shape your destiny and your perceptions will create your reality. It is very important to understand that what you *think* is basically a *mirror* of what you believe. Therefore, you must create a positive belief system. To change your beliefs, you must first get a good handle on your self-limiting beliefs so you can change them. Self-limiting beliefs will hold you back from becoming successful.

Self-limiting beliefs are those things that linger in our mind from our past. They are negative thoughts inside our heads from the past that do not serve us well, yet we continue to hold onto them. Basically, they are the limits that we impose upon *ourselves.* These limiting beliefs often come from social conditioning and the "things" that we were taught or told to us in our upbringing. They involve all the limits that were placed on us by our parents and other adults close to us and the negative concepts people told you about yourself when you were growing up, or what was told to you in an unhealthy relationship. These are the "things" that people told you that you "could not do" or "would not achieve" in your life and all of the negative labels that were placed upon you.

No one has the right to tell us what the future holds for us or "what" we can become. However, most parents and loved ones do have a way of projecting their fears and/or inadequacies onto their children, telling them what they cannot do, highlighting the negatives, and focusing only on their current situation or past misfortunes. Often times this is done out of a desire to keep the person safe; however, these negative words and images become buried in our subconscious mind and make us believe what we cannot accomplish, so we stop trying.

Unfortunately, when people tell us that we cannot do something often enough, we start to believe it and question *whether we can*. Sadly, our subconscious mind stores all of those negative events and experiences in our brain and this is how the wrong beliefs are embedded into our mind. This is why you think the way you do and/or find it so challenging to reach the level of success that you desire.

The problem lies in the way we think. Fortunately, we no longer have to accept this as our truth. We can get rid of these limiting beliefs. How, you may ask? By reprogramming our brain. We can retrain our subconscious mind by focusing all of our attention toward the things that we actually want—our dreams and desires. Then we can adopt some new beliefs and behaviors for our life. Through repetition of new words and phrases, we can dissolve the sabotaging stories and false beliefs in our mind and then focus our attention only on what we actually want for the future.

To change your belief system and start eliminating your self-limiting beliefs, you will need to *concentrate* on what you want instead of what you do not want in life. Think positive thoughts and start to practice feeling positive emotions. Know that you attract to your life whatever you give energy and attention to, whether positive or negative. Remember that what you *think* creates the *feelings* you experience.

4. *Eliminate all of your Self-Limiting Beliefs*—Here is how to eliminate your self-limiting beliefs:

   a) *Step 1: Identify* your self-limiting beliefs by answering a few basic questions: What are you fearful about? What caused these fears? What are some of the things that you believe you cannot do? Why? What do you believe is holding you back in life? What is something that resonates in your mind that a parent or teacher told you that you would never be able to do? Why are you so confrontational or why are you so passive? Do you feel inferior to other people? If so, why?

Write down your responses in a journal or notebook that you can refer to or reflect upon at a later time. Don't analyze them, just answer the questions. These limiting beliefs may not be apparent to you at first, so you may need help in identifying them. They may be lurking in your mind without your awareness. Talking with a friend or consulting with a professional may be the best way to identify them. Utilizing a psychologist or success coach like myself will allow an individual to receive more objective feedback as to the existence and severity of the problem. Once a person has identified his or her self-limiting beliefs or negative beliefs, then the person will be able to begin the healing and change process.

b) *Step 2: Simply stop believing in the negative viewpoints.* You will need to immediately start accepting and believing that these beliefs are false. Until the negative energy of these limiting beliefs is shifted, any attempts to change your mind will be blocked by your self-imposed limiting beliefs.

c) *Step 3: Get rid of your "old" mindset.* You will need to develop a *vision* for your future and empower your *vision* instead of empowering your problems. This can be accomplished by:

    i. writing down and developing specific goals,

    ii. including steps to achieve the goals, and

    iii. writing down the challenges and obstacles that may be faced by attempting to achieve these goals.

d) *Step 4:* Shift your point of view to the positive. This is a way of freeing oneself from negative thinking, negative words, and negative people.

e) *Step 5: Start believing for more and engage in positive self-talk and affirmations.* In order to design a new belief system, it will be necessary to utilize positive affirmations that are on target with what you want to have happen in your life. You start by repeating these new statements and affirmations on a daily basis. These affirmations must be true and real for you because the subconscious mind will respond to how you feel and how you think about what you are saying. So practice saying these words, "I am in the process of changing" or "I've decided to change." These positive affirmations will allow you to replace the old limiting beliefs with new positive thoughts.

   f) *Step 6: Create a new picture of success for yourself.* You should start utilizing visualization as another tool to release your limiting beliefs. This is a way to use your imagination to visualize and daydream about what it would feel like and look like to be successful. Experience in your mind what success would feel like to you.

5. *Focus only on what you actually want*—When you focus on what you want instead of what you don't want, you are training the subconscious mind to accept what you want to happen in life. In order to get your subconscious mind headed in a new direction, you should focus on what is going right in your life, thus training the mind to be more certain. You must state what you want in the positive and filter out the words "don't," "not," and "no" from your mind. Once you start to give energy to what you actually want to happen instead of what you don't want, you will begin to attract positive things to your life.

   For example, if you continue to say you don't want to be in debt, you are actually creating the picture of debt in your life and thus the vibration of lack. Therefore, you must create the opposite of what you don't want and *only* focus your mind on what you actually want. Instead, say, "I will be wealthy and successful," which in turn, will bring about the funds to pay off your debt. Once again, remember to *only* focus on what you want! You will begin to see changes in your life when your subconscious mind starts to pick up the new belief system from your conscious mind.

   So remember, a major step in the process to success is to understand that success begins and ends in the mind. The way you think will determine your level of success for your entire future. You must decide today that you will become successful and then take the appropriate steps to bring it to fruition. In order to become successful, you must step up your level of thinking to a higher level. As Mr. Jim Rohn often said, "We have to learn to work harder on ourselves than we do on our jobs. In order to have more, we have to become more; unless we change it will not change." So always be willing to develop yourself into what you want to become.

6. *Utilize the Law of Attraction*—The law of attraction states that we will attract into our lives—whether wanted or unwanted—whatever we give our energy, focus, and attention to. It is my belief that the law of attraction is just another way of utilizing the power of prayer. Prayer is communicating with your Heavenly Father and expecting results. Prayer involves a positive attitude of affirmation and participation with God's plan and purpose for us. We *must* have our thoughts centered in *faith, gratitude,* and *expectancy.* Once we pray and ask for something, we must believe with every fiber in our body that it will come to completion.

After you have asked and truly have the faith and belief that it will be answered, you must then move from believing to expecting—expect that it will happen! When you are expecting something to happen, you must abstain from any doubt. The law of attraction not only reacts to the words you use and the thoughts you think, it also responds to how you feel about what you say and how you feel about what you think. For that reason, you should begin to prepare for your desires to come into your life. Remember, if you doubt you can have it in any way, then you are blocking or pushing it away. When you do this, you are sending out contradicting messages. It is only when the contradictory thoughts, talk, and images are removed that your desired results will manifest.

Through the law of attraction, you will begin to be guided to the people, opportunities, and places that will help you achieve your goals. You will know when you are attracting this vibration because your mind will begin to automatically focus on what you want and stop being negative about what you do not want. When this happens, you will begin to see dramatic changes in your life. The three forces of power that you must use are: desire, belief, and expectation.

Wright

I understand that you teach the philosophy that we become what we think. How does this correlate with reaching our potential and achieving greatness?

Hymes

We do actually "become" what we think about. Because success is mainly a state of mind, when we regularly concentrate and focus on what we want to accomplish and back this up with positive affirmations and visualizations, we start to achieve these things; and this has been backed by scientific research. It has been proven via quantum physics that we literally become what we think about. Our thoughts, beliefs, and emotions actually shape our world.

Quantum physics is the science of possibilities! It is the science of how, what, and why everything that makes up the universe as well as everything in it—both the seen as well as the unseen—is derived. It explains how everything in our world comes into existence starting from the physical aspect of the events, conditions, and circumstances of everything in the Universe. Quantum physics is a detailed study of quantum mechanics, which determines how everything in the cosmos has come to exist, beginning at the atomic and sub-atomic levels.

Quantum mechanics breaks energy down into two forms of behavior: the wave function and particles. More simply put, it has to do with how our lives unfold and where things originated and/or were derived from, which is pure energy.

In 1925, an incredible discovery was made by Albert Einstein when he discovered that $E=mc^2$, or in other words, energy equals everything. What Einstein's world-changing discovery would prove was that these atoms could be broken down and analyzed and that subatomic particles, which collectively formed the atoms, were pure energy. If you can think back and remember a little about your science classes in elementary school, you will recall that we discovered that everything we see in the physical world is made up of molecules. So in reality, through the vessel of our attention and awareness, we can relentlessly work at manifesting into form what we want. In other words, our reality is only as real as we believe it into its appearance of solidity.

Accordingly, the more you think about and focus on something, the more you will attract that into your life. If you focus on bills, negativity, and bad health, then you will attract that to your life. Whereas, if you focus on creating opportunities, helping others, and building wealth, then you will attract positive people and resources into your life that will help you to put into place the things necessary to bring about your positive thoughts and plans. It's like the idea of planting a seed today and then waiting for the harvest tomorrow.

So if success and greatness are what you want, then success and greatness are what you need to start concentrating and thinking about. Success is a skill that can be learned by anyone who is willing to devote time and energy to gain the specialized knowledge needed in a particular desired area of concentration.

So here is the secret: people who want to become successful need to train their mind to only concentrate and think about those things that they actually want to happen in their lives. Remember, it is possible if you believe that it is achievable and within your reach. The only thing you need to do is to change your thinking and follow a plan of action.

Wright

Dr. Hymes, as you know, the impact of the downturn in the U.S. economy and the current slumping economy is causing a lot of consternation with individuals today. What strategies do you provide to help your clients keep their minds focused on the correct activities during these trying times?

Hymes

Well, one of the simple things I tell them is to keep the faith. As developing individuals, we have to learn how to keep our mind focused on the results we are looking for and not get sidetracked by the media or by the negativity we hear from other people.

If we have plans to achieve greatness, it is vitally important for us to stay focused on the results we desire in order to implement our plan. What's very important during bad economic times is to continue to take small steps toward our goals every day. When we become overwhelmed, we will still need to keep moving forward and not allow fear to take us down.

Now, this is where we will get to utilize that new strong belief system I talked about before. We have to believe that circumstances will change for the better, that better days are coming, and have faith in God that He will pull us through.

Wright

I find it strange that, in spite of situations like the current slump in the economy, there are people who are still thriving. Why do you believe that some people seem to get everything they want out of life while others struggle just to make ends meet?

Hymes

They are still struggling because they almost certainly were never taught how to be successful or how to create a success mentality. They were never given the right directions or plans to follow.

Now, think about this for a moment: we go to school to learn how to read and write. We learn as toddlers how to walk and talk, but when it actually comes down to the most important lessons of all—learning about building success and wealth—we were left without instructions or a plan of action. So the magic question is this: whose job was it to teach us about success and wealth? We certainly did not learn it in high school. Many of our parents certainly could not teach us what they did not know. Because of this, many people did not learn how to become successful or how to create a success mentality; accordingly, they are still struggling.

I was told a long time ago that God's vision for us is so much bigger than we can even imagine. All we need to do is to ask for what we desire and then put faith and action behind it, expecting it to come to materialization. It's that simple. In order to achieve greatness, we must first put it in our minds. I still believe this truth.

So in other words, if you can imagine it in your mind, then you can achieve it in reality. Successful people are people who enjoy an amazing quality of life because they took the time to learn how. They are also successful because they were willing to do a few things differently. In order to be successful, we must be willing to do things today that others are not willing to do. They were persistent in their actions. They seem to attract the things they want and desire because they practice some of the basic success philosophies.

Wright

In your book, *The Psychology of Success,* you talk about the concept of developing faith. How does this concept contribute to becoming successful?

Hymes

I believe faith is one of the key ingredients to success. It is something that one must possess if he or she expects to have any level of higher success. Faith is a very important element of success because we must believe that we are going to receive the things we desire. Unfortunately, some people tend to think of having faith only when things are going great; however, when everything appears to go haywire, they forget that they still must have unwavering faith that the situation will change for the better. Faith is confidence and the belief in something that we cannot see or something that we do not know. It is my credence that faith is our raw power because without it, nothing happens in our lives.

So when it comes to our personal growth and achieving our life dreams, faith means that we must trust and have a strong belief in a higher being to deliver our desires to us. Even when we cannot see how it will be done, we must believe that it will be done. So I encourage everyone to develop his or her faith by embracing positive thoughts and emotions. Then "lean not to your own understanding," but, rather, commit to believing that your desires will happen.

Wright

What is the success formula that you teach in your success-building seminars and motivational speeches?

Hymes

One of my mentors, Dr. Norman Vincent Peale, ended the majority of his speeches by saying, "Shoot for the moon and even if you miss, you will land among the stars." This is the type of success concept that I have adopted for myself.

The success formula that I teach in my seminars is based on my personal success model. I live by it every day and I tell myself certain things every morning via affirmations. If you don't mind, I would like to share my personal success philosophy with the readers. My personal success formula involves the following:

1. I Dream Big! I focus only on what I want to accomplish.
2. I always ask my Heavenly Father for what I desire and I developed a success mentality and a new belief system.
3. I always put action behind my desires.

4. I have a serving heart. Instead of thinking about only what I can achieve for myself, I focus on how I can help others.

5. I have cleared out all of my negative thinking and removed all of my self-limiting beliefs.

6. I believed that change will happen and waited with expectancy for manifestation.

7. I am very persistent in whatever I do.

8. I stayed optimistic and hopeful.

9. I kept a prosperous mentality.

10. I modeled myself after other successful people.

11. I concentrated on creating rather than competing.

12. I am very grateful and I remain humble.

13. I expect God's favor.

14. I keep going in spite of the obstacles that I face every day.

Wright

We hear a lot today about executive coaching, success coaching, financial coaching, and other types of one-on-one coaching. Will you explain to our readers exactly what professional coaching is and what's the difference between coaching, counseling, and therapy?

Hymes

Coaching may sound a little like therapy or counseling, but it is quite different. Although coaching is clearly therapeutic in that its aim is to enhance an individual's performance or life experience, there are significant differences between coaching and psychotherapy. Therapy usually focuses on the past, whereas coaching focuses on the future. Therapy is about resolving issues and coaching is about improvement and empowerment. Coaching is different from clinical therapy because it is about the here and now and not about the past. It is about the individual looking into the future to where he or she wants to be and the psychologist helping the person to get there.

Coaching is also not consulting, instead, skilled practitioners work with the individual to create the change he or she wants. A professional coach is someone who works with an individual to help him or her reach some high level goals.

Executive coaching is primarily used within the workplace to improve the effectiveness of an individual within a formally defined coaching agreement. Personal development coaching is used to help people get from where they are to where they want to be. Behavioral coaching focuses on observable behaviors rather than internal psychological states.

In coaching, techniques are used to help people look into the future to where they want to be rather than focusing on the past. Through a one-on-one relationship with the psychologist, coaching focuses on helping people develop their skills.

There are usually at least four major activities that occur in coaching relationships: data-gathering, feedback, implementation of the intervention (coaching), and evaluation. The aim is always sustained cognitive, emotional, and behavioral changes that facilitate goal attainment and performance enhancement.

At my firm, we primarily utilize behavior-based coaching, which is the use of validated, reliable, psychology-based tools and techniques to achieve successful and lasting behavioral change. In my practice, we also help people get to awareness; that's one of the main functions we do as professional coaches.

Some of the areas where coaching helps individuals to grow and develop are in the following areas:

1. Determining what's holding them back from success.
2. Shaping what their blind spots are.
3. Clarifying their true potential and purpose in life.
4. Helping them to meet and/or exceed major corporate objectives.
5. Helping individuals to create their success plan and work on behaviors and habits that are counterproductive to reaching a high level of success.

One-on-one professional coaching actually helps to bring focus to a person. It is about enhancing performance or illuminating one's positive life experiences rather than treating dysfunctions.

Wright

Well, what a great conversation. I really appreciate all this time you've spent with me talking about this extremely important subject—a subject I'm sure our readers will find that you know a lot about.

Hymes

Thank you for allowing me to share what I am so passionate about—helping others to grow, develop, and succeed in life. In parting, here are some final words to think about: "Action is a great restorer and builder of confidence. Inaction is not only the result, but the cause, of fear. Perhaps the action you take will be successful; perhaps different action or adjustments will have to follow. But any action is better than no action at all"—Dr. Norman Vincent Peale. Learn to "work harder on yourself than you do on your job"—Mr. Jim Rohn. "Yes You Can," *be* whatever you want to become. Never stop chasing your dreams!

Wright

Today we've been talking with Dr. Amy Hymes. She is president of a highly successful management consulting and training company where she consults on workforce planning and the people side of business. She successfully assists organizations with building a strong corporate culture. Dr. Hymes trains, coaches, motivates, and helps develop executives, managers, and key employees all around the globe.

Dr. Hymes, thank you so much for being with us today on *Yes You Can!*

Hymes

Thank you for having me.

Dr. Amy Hymes is an organizational psychologist focusing on the development of individuals, teams, and organizations. She has a strong commitment to "people development" and specializes in enhancing the minds of others via training workshops, speaking engagements, and self-improvement products. Dr. Amy is a student of human potential and a leader on a mission to assist others with reaching their self-actualization. She thrives on helping individuals with self-improvement in order to develop pathways to success. With more than twenty years of progressive human resources management and corporate and military expertise, Dr. Hymes has executive level experience encompassing a range of human capital management disciplines. She has directed the organizational growth and implementation of human resources strategies, policies, and programs covering training and succession planning, staffing and recruitment, compensation and benefits administration, performance management and employee relations, and employment law compliance. Dr. Hymes demonstrates expertise with providing executive level coaching to enhance an organization's human capital development strategies, leadership training to gain management and emotional intelligence skills, and one-on-one coaching to facilitate behavior change and goal attainment. Her capabilities also involve developing teams and helping them to work collaboratively in order to exceed organizational growth objectives. This is usually accomplished through team-building events, anger management coaching sessions, and/or conflict resolution interventions. Dr. Amy is solution-focused and her strong relationship management and interpersonal skills help to build rapport and trust throughout any group or organization. Her definite purpose in life is to motivate, educate, and train others on how to develop a success mentality and reach their goals in life. If you are interested in learning more about the topics shared by Dr. Hymes in this chapter, please reserve your copy of her next book to be released in spring 2010 titled, *The*

Psychology of Reaching Abundant Success: How to re-train your mind to reach any goal, overcome any limiting belief, and live a prosperous life. You will be intrigued by the knowledge you will gain from reading and learning how to apply the concepts taught in the next more than twelve-chapter book. To learn more of the success strategies taught by Dr. Hymes, you can also tune into her national professional development radio talk show that airs on Voice America Radio and WEBR Radio. In addition, Dr. Amy is the host and executive producer of a new self-improvement television talk show called *Inspiring Moments: The Dr. Amy Show,* which will be airing in spring 2010 on Fairfax, Virginia, public access Channel 10.

Dr. Hymes is available for consulting engagements; leadership, management, and supervisor training classes; personal development success-building weekend seminars; and keynote speeches for corporations, schools, associations, high school and college graduations, and community organizations on a local, national, and international basis.

Amy J. Hymes, PhD

Hymes & Associates Consulting Group
Human Resources Consulting & Training Services
P.O. Box 4034
Woodbridge, Virginia
703-873-7086
dramy@amyhymes.com
www.hymesandassociates.com
www.amyhymes.com

CHAPTER 9

A Special Interview

by Jim Rohn

David E. Wright (Wright)

I join the millions of people whose lives were changed by the teachings of Jim Rohn and remember him for the wisdom he unselfishly shared with people all over the world for more than four decades. I always looked forward with excitement to our conversations because I knew that he would be interested, engaged, and always informative. He was the perfect conversationalist. Jim Rohn died of pulmonary embolism on December 5, 2009, at the age of seventy-nine. Jim's courage in his final months was a testament to the messages he shared with the world. He was truly an original and I will miss him.

It's my sincere pleasure today to welcome Jim Rohn to *Yes You Can*. Jim helped motivate and train an entire generation of personal development trainers, as well as hundreds of executives from America's top corporations. He's been described as everything from a "master motivator" to a "modern day Will Rodgers," to a legend. Jim has been internationally hailed over the years as one of the most influential thinkers of our time. His professional development seminars have spanned thirty-nine years. During his lifetime, he addressed more than six thousand audiences and four million people worldwide. He has authored seventeen books as well as dozens of audio and video programs. There simply are not enough superlatives when introducing Jim Rohn.

Jim, thank you for taking time to visit with us today.

Jim Rohn (Rohn)

Hey, my pleasure.

Wright

Before we dive into some pretty deep subjects, I know our readers would appreciate an update on your focus at the time of this interview.

Rohn

Well, I'm still involved in world travel—from Asia to South Africa, South America, to Europe, across the United States—which I've been doing for the last forty years and enjoying it very much.

Wright

I've belonged to a political discussion group called Great Decisions, for the last fifteen years. Every year we discuss conditions in Africa and every year we come away with our hands in our pockets, saying we don't know what can be done about it. Is it as bad as we believe?

Rohn

It's a complex continent and who knows what it will finally take. You know, there are some good signs but you're right.

Wright

The problems are just voluminous.

Rohn

I have lectured in all the major cities in South Africa. I've gone there several times over the last twenty years. When I first went they still had Apartheid, now that's all gone. There are some good signs that recovery is under way and I love to see that.

I first lectured in Moscow in Russia, starting about ten years ago and fortunately that was after the walls came tumbling down—they were changing from communism to capitalism. I've made about five lecture tours in Russia in the last ten years, teaching capitalism and personal responsibility and entrepreneurship. It's exciting to go back and see so many of them doing it. They still have a long way to go—there's still push and pull between the old ways and the new ways.

Years and years ago when I went to South America, every country had a dictator. Now they're all gone, for the most part. So there are a lot of improvements that have been made around the world but there is still a long way to go.

Wright

Do you appreciate the United States when you come back?

Rohn

No doubt about it. This is the place where you can start with so little and make your fortune with some good advice and coaching and a bit of training and personal responsibility and a whole lot of courage. That's extraordinary.

Wright

I spend a lot of time with professionals from all types of industries and I often give career advice when I'm asked.

Would you mind looking back over your career and sharing a story or two that demonstrates some relevant success principles? In other words, to what do you attribute your success in life?

Rohn

I met someone when I was twenty-five; his name was Earl Schoff (this is in most of my recordings and writings). I worked for him for five years. He died at the early age of forty-nine, but during those five years I worked for him, he gave me really a lot of the fundamentals—especially the economic and personal development principles—that revolutionized my life.

When I met him I had only pennies in my pocket, nothing in the bank, and creditors calling once in a while saying, "You told us the check was in the mail." That embarrasses me.

I think what triggered my search to find him was what I call "the Girl Scout story." I was at home alone and heard a knock on my door. I go to the door and there's this Girl Scout selling cookies. She gives me this great presentation (it's the best organization in the world). She goes on and on and she describes the several different flavors available and that the cost is only two dollars. Then she politely asked me to buy.

No problem, I wanted to buy—big problem, I didn't have two dollars. I can remember today that embarrassing moment—I'm a grown man and I'm twenty-five years old; I've had one year of college, I've got a little family started, I live in America, and I don't have two dollars in my pocket.

I didn't want to tell her that, so I lied to her and said, "Hey look, we've already bought lots of Girl Scout cookies, we've still got plenty in the house we haven't eaten yet.

She said, "Oh, that's wonderful! Thank you very much," and she leaves.

When she leaves, I say to myself, "I don't want to live like this anymore. I mean, how low you can get, lying to a Girl Scout? That's got to be the bottom, right?

I called it "the day that turns your life around." Everybody can look back at some of those days when you made a unique decision at a particular time and you were never the same again. That was one of those days.

Shortly after that I met this incredible mentor I went to work for—Earl Schoff. Using the things he taught me, I became a millionaire by the age of thirty-two.

It doesn't take much if you get the right information and put it to work and are willing to accept refinement, keep up your studies, and engage primarily in what we call "personal development"—becoming more valuable. For economics, personal development makes you more valuable to the marketplace. Personal development also makes you become more valuable as a father, a mother, a parent, a friend, a business colleague, and as a citizen.

Personal development is the subject I have talked most about seeing how valuable you can be to yourself, to your community, and to those around you.

I've got a little economic phrase I use that says, "We get paid for bringing value to the marketplace." And the first part of that is the value you bring, such as a product; but the biggest part of what you bring is how valuable you become through personal development. I say, "To climb the ladder of success, work harder on yourself than you do on your job." If you work hard on your job, you can make a living; if you work hard on yourself, you can make a fortune.

I learned those very fundamental ideas when I was twenty-five. Fortunately I discovered them at twenty-five rather than at fifty-five. Fifty-five is okay and seventy-five is still okay but gosh, it's good to learn them at the age of twenty-five when you can really put them to work. These ideas revolutionized my life and they formed the foundation of what I've shared now all these years in so many forms.

Wright

I've only heard the name Schoff twice. You just mentioned it and when I was in junior high school in seventh and eighth and ninth grades, one of my mentors was a coach named Schoff. He was a real mentor. This guy was just a fine, fine, man.

Rohn

The same man, Earl Schoff, influenced Mary Kay (the lady who started Mary Kay Cosmetics) and me back in 1955–1956. Those were the early, early years. Mary Kay went on to become a superstar. What he shared with me just transformed my life.

Wright

You're known throughout the world as a personal development expert. In practical terms, what does that really mean?

Rohn

Well, there's a phase that says, "Success is not something you pursue, success is something you attract"—by becoming an attractive person. Currently I'm sharing it like this: to really do well you need multiple skills. If you've just got one skill, it's too risky economically. For example, a guy has worked for a company for twenty years and the division he works for goes out of business. He's lost his job and he tells us he's in financial trouble. The reason is that, even after twenty years of working, he only had one skill. If he had taken an accounting course or some other course two nights a week he would have had another skill to market. There's so much available out there that can increase your value to the marketplace.

I started learning these extra skills: finding good people, sales, finding a product I could believe in and talk about its merits until somebody said Yes, then follow up and get referrals. Then I learned to build an organization. I then learned organization—getting people to work together. I needed to learn to get a team and work together. Then I learned recognition—I learned to reward people for small steps of progress.

The biggest skill I learned was communication. I got involved in training, showing people how the job works, and then I got involved in teaching. I taught setting goals, personal development leadership, and communication skills. My theme for that was, "You need both job skills and life skills," because just learning how to set goals revolutionized my life.

Then the ultimate in communication is learning to inspire—helping people see themselves as better than they are, transport them in to the future, paint the possibilities, and then use your own testimony. Say, "Hey, if I can do it, you can do it."

So you're starting with pennies, you're behind, the creditors are calling; but that's not really what's important. What's important is the decision today to start the journey of self-improvement. I think that theme has been paramount in all of my teaching and training during the last forty years—work harder on yourself than you do on your job.

In leadership, I teach that to attract attractive people, you must be attractive. So it's a constant pursuit of self-development and personal development.

The theme during my career, teaching, and training during the past forty years is: communication, managing your time, managing your money, and learning to inspire.

Wright

You know, I have my own opinion about how difficult it is for people to change, whether it involves a health issue or dieting, for example. Do you believe that people can really change and why is change so difficult?

Rohn

Give easy steps. For example, if you want to change your health and you say, "I've got to do something that will make me healthy. My momma taught that an apple a day was healthy," why not start there?

If you don't start with something simple, you can forget the rest of the complicated stuff. Sometimes it's good to do it with someone else. I've found in all my entrepreneurial business projects during the last forty years, it's more inspiring to say, "Let's go do it," than to say, "I'm going to go do it." Get together with someone and say, "Let's get healthy, let's exercise, let's go to the gym, let's climb a mountain." The "let's" is what's very powerful. A lot of things are pretty tough to do all by yourself.

Wright

In the past there've been some major scandals in corporate America. I know you've counseled many high profile executives throughout the years. Is there a leadership crisis in America? What do you think has contributed to this kind of moral failure?

Rohn

No, it's always been such from the beginning of recorded history, when there were just four people on Earth. You know there was the great scandal of brother who killed brother (Cain and Abel). So it's not a current phenomenon—it's not a twenty-first century phenomenon. Even the Old Testament records good kings and bad kings—those who "did right in the sight of the Lord" and those who led the people into idolatry. You know, it's just not unusual.

My best explanation is the "great adventure" started ages ago, according to the Storyteller. God created all these angels and then gave them the dignity of choice, and a third of them decided to go with Lucifer and make a run on God's throne. They didn't win, but it started what I call "the adventure of the Creator and the spoiler." And then I further describe it with the concept that the adventure of our life seems to be that opposites are in conflict and we are in the middle. But this is what makes a great adventure.

Illness tries to overcome your health, but if you work on your health you can overcome your illness. If, however, you let up the least little bit, sure enough, illness creeps up and takes away some more of your health.

Regarding liberty and tyranny in the world, for a while there was more tyranny than liberty. Since the walls came down in Berlin I am hopeful that there will be more liberty than tyranny in the future.

But whether its politics or whether it's corporations, it doesn't matter, the temptation is always there—the drama is always there. Should we do the right thing or would it be okay to cross the line? I use the following illustration sometimes: When I was a little kid I saw a cartoon of a little boy. The little boy had an angel—a little angel—on one shoulder, and a little devil on the other shoulder. Both of them were whispering in his ear. The little devil said, "Go ahead and do it, it will be okay."

The little angels says, "No, no, it *won't* be okay."

The little devil says, "Yes, yes, go ahead, it's okay; nobody will know."

The little angel says, "No, no, no!"

That little cartoon appeared back when I was a kid. It describes the concept of opposites in conflict and that's what makes an adventure.

There wouldn't be positive without negative, it doesn't seem like. And you couldn't win if you couldn't lose. If you took a football today and walked out to the stadium (and we followed you) and in the football stadium you took the football and walked across the goal line, would we all cheer and call it a touchdown? The answer is No, that's silly. It's not a touchdown until you face the three-hundred-pounders. If you can muscle past them (they want to smash your face in the dirt) and if you can dance by the secondary, on a special day, we call it a touchdown, and maybe you win the championship.

That's the deal—opposites are in conflict. We're tempted every day, whether it's the little things or something big and major. You come to the intersection and the light is yellow and it starts to turn red. Some little voice may whisper to you, "Go ahead, you're late—you can make it." But if you try running that light you may wind up dead. If you say, "No, I'll be more cautious," then you live a little bit longer.

So it's not that we're not involved in this push and pull. It happens at the high echelons of corporate America. Little voices whisper in a collective way around the boardroom, and the board members decide to cross the line. They think, "It looks like we can get by with it—we can put it off-shore or we can play some games here and we'll be okay" or "If we want this stock to grow and necessity demands it, we probably skate the line a little bit."

That happens in the poorest of homes and it happens in the richest of homes. It happens in the boardroom and it happens on Main Street and it happens in the back alley. So it doesn't really matter where it is, temptation is always there. But that's what makes the adventure—to see if you can handle the temptation and do more right than wrong and have a longer list of virtues than mistakes; then you win.

Wright

I once read an article you wrote about attitude. In it you said attitude determines how much of the future we're allowed to see. This is a fascinating thing to say. Will you elaborate on this thought?

Rohn

Well, it's attitude about four things:

1. *How you feel about the past.* Some people carry the past around like a burden. They continually live and dwell on their past mistakes. They live in the past (i.e., their past failures) and it just drains away all the energy they could apply to something much more positive. We have to have a good healthy attitude about the past. The key on that is just to learn from it— "Hey, here's where I messed up, I've got that corrected now, and I'm going to make the changes for the future." We call that "drawing on the past" as a good school of experience to make corrections in errors in judgment or whatever put you in a bad place.

2. *How you feel about the future.* We need to look back for experience but we need to look ahead for inspiration. We need to be inspired by the goals we set for ourselves and for our family, the goals we've set for friendship, lifestyle, becoming wealthy, powerful, and influential. As a unique citizen, each of us needs to be inspired by those goals that get us up early and keep us up late, fire up the fuel of our imagination, and how can we accomplish them.

3. *How you feel about everybody.* You can't succeed by yourself. It takes everybody for each of us to be successful. Each of us needs all of us. One person doesn't make an economy; one person doesn't make a symphony orchestra. So you have to have that unique sense of the value of everybody and that it really does take everybody for any one person to be successful.

4. *How you feel about yourself.* This is the most important one. At the end of the day, evaluate yourself—"I pushed it to the limit, I did everything I could, I made every call, I stretched as far as I could." If that's true, then you can lie down and sleep a good sleep. Solomon wrote, "The sleep of the laboring man is

sweet . . ." (Ecclesiastes 5:12). This describes people who put in the work—who work hard either with their hands or with their mind or with their ability to communicate, whatever it is—so at the end of the day they feel good about themselves. Nothing is more powerful than high self-esteem. It builds self-confidence, which builds success.

Those four attitudes really do give you a promising look at the future. But if you're always being pulled back by the past or distracted because you find it difficult to manage your life with people you have to associate with, that's tough. And the better you can handle that and realize the law of averages says you're going to be around some good people and some bad people, and you're going to be around some ambitious people and some not so ambitious, the better off you'll be. You've got to learn to take it all in stride.

Then knowing that you're on track for better health and you're on track for becoming financially independent is part of the equation. You haven't quite got it solved, but you're on track for the management of your time and your money. And your attitude toward that really creates high inspiration that the future's going to multiply several times better than the past.

Wright

I don't normally like to frame a question in the negative but I thought it would be interesting to get your perspective on mistakes that people make in life and in business. If you had to name the top three on a list of mistakes people make that kept them from succeeding or living a fulfilled life, what would they be?

Rohn

Well, number one mistake economically is not to understand that people can make you wealthy. And all you have to do is just figure out how to do that. For example: Johnny mows Mrs. Brown's lawn and she pays five dollars. One day it occurs to him, "If I get my friend Paul to mow this lawn, Mrs. Brown would pay five dollars. I would give Paul four dollars and keep one for myself because I got the job." Instantly Johnny has now moved to a higher level of economics that says this is how you become wealthy.

A little phrase that philosophically and economically changed my life is: "Profits are better than wages." Wages make you a living but profits make you a fortune. You don't have to be General Motors, you don't have to be high in the industrial complex society to understand this concept; that's why it's so powerful to teach capitalism, how to buy and sell and how to sell and buy.

I've got so many stories of people I've helped in my seminars who started with pennies and now they're rich. That's the key—learning how to employ other people. First do it yourself—learn how to do it yourself—then find a need someone has and get someone else to render the service, and then someone else and then someone else. Teach them the same, and the principles of economics and capitalism. The knowledge of how to go from having pennies to gaining a fortune is so simple.

When I taught it to the Russians they couldn't believe how simple it was. I said, "Capital is any value you set aside to be invested in an enterprise that brings value to the marketplace hoping to make a profit"—that's capitalism. They couldn't believe I could put it in one sentence.

Wright

I can't either.

Rohn

I teach kids how to have two bicycles—one to ride and one to rent. It doesn't take long to make a profit. If you're halfway bright, if you get just a little advice to give you a chance to start, you'll make it.

I see capitalism in two parts—one is capital time, the other is capital money. If you wisely learn to invest capital money you can make a fortune. And then together with that, if you can learn to invest capital time you can also amass a fortune. You set aside time to be invested in an enterprise.

I started that part-time when I was twenty-five years old, all those years ago in 1955. I took about fifteen to twenty hours a week part-time and invested it in a capital enterprise. By the time I was thirty-two I was a millionaire. It didn't take much money because I only invested $200, which I borrowed. That was my capital money, but the other was my capital time. Once I learned how to invest both and then learned how to teach and train and inspire other people to do the same, it totally changed my life.

I don't have to worry about social security—I developed my own social security. It's interesting that they're not teaching that today when social security is such a main topic. We've got to let our young people put aside some of that withholding and put it in a personal account. How about teaching them how to be financially independent? Who's doing that? John Kennedy said, "Don't ask what your country can do for you . . ." Don't ask what the social security program can do for you, why not ask what you can do for your country—or social security? Could I mow Mrs. Brown's lawn and collect five dollars and do it part-time? I could then get someone else to do it and then someone else to do another job, and finally work my way from the pennies in my pocket to the fortune that I could have because this is America—the land of opportunity.

It's startling how simple it is in concept and how really easy it is in practice; but the results can be phenomenal. I got such great early results that I never did look back, from age twenty-five until today.

For me it's fun to teach it. I've been teaching it now for all these years and I've got some testimonials where I helped people start, just like I started with pennies, and now they're rich. It's just exciting.

One of the great exciting experiences is to have your name appear in somebody's testimonial: "Here's the person who found me, here's the person who taught me, here's the person who wouldn't let me quit, gave me more reasons for staying than for leaving. Here's the person who believed in me until I could believe in myself," then they mention your name. I call that big time, and you can't buy it with money. You have to simply earn it by sharing ideas with people that make a difference in their life. And I love to do it.

Wright

This is the definition of great mentors.

Rohn

Yes, I love to be that. Hopefully my books and tapes and my personal appearances have done that throughout the years.

Wright

I'd like to go back to the issue of personal development and change. Considering the issues most Americans face in this modern era with all of our technology, where would you advise most people to focus their energy if they could only change one thing about themselves?

Rohn

I'd advise them to start figuring out to how to learn another skill, and then another skill. Then it would be good to learn another language. People who know more than one language receive good pay. Some of my business colleagues who speak three or four languages make three or four million a year. Not that this is a guarantee, but that's just an idea for self-improvement. Learn something beyond what you know now because it could be something that you can cash in on, maybe sooner than you think.

Wright

Not to mention the fact that you're talking for the first time to another whole culture and look what you could learn. I've always been fascinated by the Chinese culture.

Rohn

I would also suggest that people develop wise use of their time and then wise use of their money. I teach kids to not spend more than seventy cents out of every dollar—ten cents for charity or church, ten cents for active capital (e.g., the two bicycles, one to ride and one to rent concept), then passive capital of 10 percent. Let someone else use it (you provide the capital that will pay you dividends, increase in stock, or whatever). I call it "seventy-ten-ten and ten." Then I teach not to buy the second car until you've bought the second house. Cars won't make you rich but houses will make you rich. I love to teach that.

A lady called me from Mexico not long ago and said, "Mr. Rohn, I'm now shopping for my third car because I just finished paying for my third house." She started listening to my training ten years ago. She not only uses it, she teaches it. Down in Mexico she makes about $40,000 a month, which is just staggering.

But it's fun—it's been fun for me over the years to have stories like that. I use my own story as an inspiration not only for myself but also for the people who listen to my lectures. And then it's fun to watch people actually grab hold of something and turn it into success.

Wright

Jim, it's been a sincere joy having this enlightening conversation with you today. I really appreciate and thank you so much again for taking the time to be with me.

Rohn

I appreciate it also and I thank you for calling.

Jim Rohn was a philosopher, motivational counselor, business executive, and best-selling author. He has been recognized as the greatest motivational speaker of all time. He was one of the world's most sought-after success counselors and business philosophers. Some of his most thought-provoking topics include: sales and entrepreneurial skills, leadership, sales and marketing, success, and personal development.

Jim Rohn conducted seminars for many years and addressed more than six thousand audiences and four million people worldwide. He was a recipient of the 1985 National Speakers Association CPAE Award. He authored more than seventeen books, audio, and video programs. Rohn has been internationally hailed over the years as one of the most influential thinkers of our time.

Revealing contemporary success secrets in a way that is both accessible and practical, Jim ignited enthusiasm and a can-do attitude in all who heard him speak. He approached the subjects of personal and professional success by asking four questions: Why? Why not? Why not you? Why not now? He answered these questions and revealed practical, perceptive secrets for success and productivity. His special style, laced with witticisms and anecdotes, captivates listeners.

Jim Rohn
www.jimrohn.com

CHAPTER 10

An Amazing Discovery— The Most Important Ingredient in Success

by Earl Davis, Jr.

David Wright (Wright)

Today we're talking with Earl Davis. Earl is a powerful and passionate speaker and success coach who is sought after by organizations such as Hilton Hotels, IBM, the United States Army, numerous schools, colleges, and trade organizations. He is the creator and host of the television program *The Winners Circle*. His company, Create Winners Inc., works with corporate professionals, entrepreneurs, small business owners, network marketers, not-for-profits, and with individuals who want to bring out the best in themselves and others.

Earl Davis, welcome to *Yes You Can!*

Earl Davis (Davis)

Good morning David, and thank you.

Wright

I understand that the title *Yes You Can!* has a special meaning to you. Would you tell our readers what that meaning is and why it's special?

Davis

Before we begin, I want to say I feel GREAT this morning, and that I'm glad to be a part of this project. GREAT to me is an acronym that stands for Getting Real Excited About Today, and I'm very excited about today because the American Dream is alive and well. I say this because more people are going to make more money in the years ahead than has been made in the last two hundred years. This is all because our economy has "hockey-sticked"—it has actually grown by three trillion dollars in the last five years alone. All of that money is running through someone's hands. Your job, my job—our job—is to make sure that some of that money runs through *our* hands and it sticks.

So this *Yes You Can!* project hopefully will share with people ways in which they can do that and capitalize during this season of opportunity.

As for the words "yes you can," the special meaning to me is this: About a year ago, my wife and I had the opportunity to travel with the entourage of President Barack Obama (at that time he was a U.S. Senator). He was coming to Tampa, Florida, during his presidential campaign. It was an exciting time. We went into the stadium and there were some fifteen thousand people who had come to see and hear his campaign message about change the American people could believe in. He also shared how he saw the world and what he felt America needed to become the leading force it once was. The mood of the moment was such a transformative time for a lot of people and for many reasons.

As U.S. president-elect Barack Obama gave his acceptance speech from Grant Park in Chicago, Illinois, I was at home watching on television with my son who was four years old at that time. As I listened to President Obama talk about his journey and that this historic election was a defining moment, tears began rolling down my cheeks. My son looked up at me and said, "Daddy, why are you crying? Are you sad, Daddy?"

"No son," I replied, "I'm not sad."

"Then why are you crying?"

"Because I'm happy. You see, son, when I was your age, having the opportunity or even thinking about a person of color being in the most powerful office in the world was farfetched, an unrealistic expectation, not a part of my consciousness, and not in the realm of my wildest imagination."

So for us to see, regardless of political affiliations and party politics, a person of color in the most powerful office in the world is an amazing feat and a testimony to the fact that we live in a world where anything is possible. And for me, that's what this *Yes You Can!* book project is all about. I remember hearing people in the stadium chant, *"Yes we can! Yes we can!"* It spoke to me on so many levels.

When I hear the title *Yes You Can!* today, as you speak it, David, it reminds me of the simple yet powerful truth of the potential that lies within and the infinite possibilities that are without. Oliver Wendell Holmes said it best, "What lies behind me and what lies before me are but tiny matters compared to what lies within me." All things are truly possible if we can just believe.

Wright

So what is the secret, if any, to creating an extraordinary quality of life?

Davis

It seems like a secret, but it really is not. It is common sense but not common practice. Most psychologists and leading thought experts agree that whatever we focus on we tend to attract. Focusing on unimportant things is a recipe for stress, but focusing on the things that really matter is the secret to creating an extraordinary quality of life.

An extraordinary quality of life, to me, requires mastering two skills: the science of achievement and the art of fulfillment. Fulfillment is an art form because success is such an elusive thing for so many people. For almost seventeen years now, I've worked with so many people and I've seen and heard so many stories about people who have struggled throughout their whole lives to "make it." When they "make it" you would think that they would be happy with everything they have achieved but they aren't; they feel unfulfilled. My perception is that success without fulfillment is failure.

I remember reading the other day, David, about this model who was working with a very prestigious magazine. She was a successful cover model, yet she jumped off her apartment building in New York. She'd just received one of the largest contracts she had ever received in her life. She was on the cover of several magazines. Exteriorly, all these "great" things were happening for this model, but internally, from her vantage point, she perceived a very different reality.

What would cause this twenty-year-old *Vogue* cover model to jump from her upscale Manhattan apartment building, taking her life? We don't know. Apparently, internally she was not fulfilled and now another beautiful spirit is gone. So to me that's what the secret to creating an extraordinary life is—achievement *and* fulfillment. Fulfillment means experiencing tremendous joy in the process. You feel not only the pleasure and excitement of the pursuit but you also feel the enthusiasm and gratitude for the little things in life along the way.

Wright

Mindset is important. How does one break away from the "hostage mindset" that you often speak about?

Davis

It was Jean Baudrillard, French philosopher, who said, "Neither dead nor alive the hostage is suspended by an incalculable outcome. It is not his destiny that awaits for him nor his own death, but anonymous chance, which can seem absolutely arbitrary. He is in a state of radical emergency, of virtual extermination."

On November 1, 1994, I was working in a fast-food restaurant. My manager and I were taking inventory in the back room. At approximately 8:30 PM I remember hearing a voice that said, "Call 911!" I turned around to hear the voice that startled me, and to my surprise, I was looking down the barrel of a loaded gun—a Glock 9 millimeter was pointed at my head! My whole body went numb. My heart felt like it left my chest and hit the floor, bounced up, and lodged in my throat. I felt like my stomach was on a continuous freefall. My whole body was just numb. It's been said that in life-and-death situations your life flashes before you, but I've got to be honest, I don't remember any of that. What I remember is all the promises I had made and hadn't kept. I remembered all the people I had hurt. I remembered the goals and dreams I had that might never come to pass. I thought about the family I wanted to start. I thought about the flashes of brilliance and greatness I felt, but because of fear, insecurity, and doubt I had never acted on those things and, therefore, I never manifested those things.

Oliver Wendell Holmes said, "Many people die with their music still in them. Why is this so? Too often it is because they are always getting ready to live." The idea of breaking away from a hostage mindset has to do with what Elizabeth Browning talked about when she wrote about "releasing the imprisoned splendor." That's what this *Yes You Can!* project is designed to do. It's designed to help people release the greatness that is within them.

How you break away from a hostage mindset is that you take your hostage thinking and you transform it into "possibility consciousness." In my situation, I was held hostage by a gunman for a couple of hours, but there are many people who will read this book who are being held hostage as well, but not by a gun. They are being held hostage by their own negative thinking. Their own negative thought life is what holds them captive and limited beyond belief.

The process of taking hostage thinking and transforming it into possibility consciousness starts with understanding what things mean. "Consciousness" is one's awareness and "possibilities" are an indication of what can be. So when you become aware of what can be, passion awakens within you. Passion has an explosive force like that of dynamite and can blow things out and virtually push one to the next level.

Wright

So after one overcomes a hostage mindset, how does one manifest and bring to reality the dreams in the heart?

Davis

Oh, that's a great question. Many people have dreams and that's one thing, but it's another thing to turn those dreams into a reality.

There are three things that make up the actual process of manifesting the dream. You need a dream, you need a team, and you need a scheme. Now, I don't like to use the word "scheme" because one definition of the word is "a devious plan," but I needed a word that rhymed. When I say "scheme" I mean a plan. PLAN is an acronym for Preparation, Leverage, Action-strategy, and Network. So if you have your dream, you have your team, and you have your scheme (plan), you can turn any dream into a reality.

Wright

According to your success methodology, there are seven positions that need filling on every team. Would you tell our readers what they are?

Davis

Yes, definitely. First of all, a dream is very important to have. Earl Nightingale said, "To achieve happiness, we should make certain that we are never without an important goal." Having a dream is a must. I truly believe that dreams are illustrations from the book your soul is writing about you. In fact, Napoleon Hill, author of the mega bestseller, *Think and Grow Rich,* said that dreams are the starting point of all worthwhile achievement. The dream is conceived from within. If cultivated properly, the dream will then become the focus of one's life. After an individual becomes cognizant of the dream, then a team is needed to materialize the dream.

I spend a lot of time with great achievers—I study the behaviors, processes, and the results of great achievers. I've adopted my method from what I've learned and seen from these great men and women who are out there achieving their goals and dreams and enjoying the process.

The first position that needs filling on everyone's team is a banker.

The second position is an attorney. The specific type of attorney needed is a tax attorney and/or intellectual property attorney. This type of attorney knows all the rules. It's one thing to make a fortune, it's another thing to keep and protect a fortune. These attorneys can help you insulate yourself and protect yourself. Ellen Stifler is a friend of mine who has a program called "BulletProofYour Business." It's an excellent program. For those who are looking for attorneys for their team, they can get a lot of great information from her Web site: www.stieflerlaw.com or by stopping by www.businessattorneydirectory.com.

The third position that needs filling on your team is a public relations specialist. This person can help you with all major media outlets that can help you convey your message, your dream, and your goals to the public in a highly concentrated way (www.prtakeoff.com or www.getfreepublicity.com).

The fourth position that needs filling is a grant writer. This year alone the United States is releasing $500 billion dollars in government funds to U.S. citizens. The government doesn't advertise to the general public, so when you find out about these government programs and you want to pursue and qualify for a government grant, it's hard to do it on your own. If you have a grant writer, the grant writer can help ease the process.

The fifth position that you want on your team is a pastor or a community leader.

The sixth position is a graphic designer.

The seventh position is a spokesperson, someone who can be the face and voice for your cause. If you're looking for a spokesperson and have not found one, use the contact information listed at the end of this interview. I'd love to help you find the spokesperson you need for your success campaign.

Wright

That's great information. What are the five tools to help you stay on track?

Davis

I share these tools with my clients and the people I work with on a regular basis. The first tool that's important to success is *Discipline*. You must make discipline a major force in your life. It was Socrates who said that the undisciplined life is not worth living, so you must have discipline.

The second tool is *Resourcefulness*. Right now, more than any other time with everything that is happening in the economy, most experts are calling this the greatest economic crisis since the Great Depression. However, when an individual is resourceful, one's focus changes and the individual will see what was not seen before. For example, let's examine the word "crisis." In the Chinese culture, the word "crisis" has two meanings. The first meaning is danger, but the second meaning is opportunity. You see, your focus is your choice. That's why the Book of Life (the Bible) says ". . . choose you this day . . ." (Joshua 24:15). So in order to take advantage of these economic opportunities you must be resourceful because the old methods aren't working anymore.

I have a friend who was going after a substantially large contract in a very competitive metropolitan area. My friend was attempting to set a presentation appointment with the CEO of the company she wanted to receive the contract award from, but she couldn't reach him no matter how many calls she made or e-mails and facsimiles she sent out. I'm sure those of you in the sales profession reading this book can relate to what my friend was going through. Most people who make numerous calls without so much as a callback would have given up, but not my friend—she got resourceful.

My friend was determined to get this contract, so she thought to herself: *what can I do*? This thought held center stage in her mind for many days. Then one day, the answer came. My friend went to a shoe store. She bought a very nice, Italian-cut leather shoe, and she only bought one pair. She only put one shoe in a box. She put her information inside the box, wrapped it up, and sent it to this CEO.

The CEO received the package. Most people like to receive gifts, so he was excited about it. He opened the box but he just saw one shoe. David, the CEO thought that this has to be the dumbest gift he has ever received. "Just one shoe—where's the other one?" he thought. "I've got two feet, I need two shoes." So he took the shoe and tossed it down. Then a note fluttered out that read: *"Now that I've got my foot in the door, allow me to introduce myself to you."* It was such a resourceful thing that she did. My friend ended up getting a $25-million-dollar contract, 25 percent of which was hers for closing the deal. I've always loved that story because it shows the reward of resourcefulness.

The next tool is *Education*. I teach in my seminars and private coaching sessions that education is the key to compensation. A lot of times people don't spend time educating themselves about their dreams, about the possibilities for their lives, or their lifestyle or healthcare choices. So you have to spend time getting the education necessary for your journey— whether it's traditional or nontraditional or by way of what Zig Ziglar calls "Automobile University." The information obtained can condense the learning curve and help individuals save money in the process. Nightingale Conant is a very good company (www.nightingale.com) as well as Labyrinth Books (www.labyrinthbooks.com).

The next tool is *Ambition*. You must have ambition if you expect to say yes to your potential. Johann Wolfgang von Goethe said, "Dream no small dreams for they have no power to move the hearts of men."

A friend of mine recently broke up with his girlfriend. I asked him why they broke up. He said he thought it was because he didn't have the assets that other guys who were pursuing her had. A few days later, I ran into the young lady, who also happened to be my friend. I asked her if it was true— that she left my friend because of his lack of assets.

"No," she replied, "that's not true. I didn't leave him because he didn't have anything—I left him because he didn't want anything."

So you must have ambition.

Then last tool is *Motivation*. You must have the "Go Power" to get up and do what is necessary to convert those dreams and possibilities into reality. But what gives you the motivation? I believe the answer is reasons. I teach that reasons will take you where motivation cannot keep you. So you must find the reasons that will give you the "Go Power" to take action and say yes to your potential.

Wright

Bill Gates once said that Microsoft is always two years away from failure. What do you recommend our readers do to stay away from business failure?

Davis

That's an important question. I look at what Bill Gates has accomplished with Microsoft. He has something like a 90 percent market share, and he fears becoming irrelevant. What should businesspeople be thinking about? Regardless of the success you may experience today, if a person who is in business becomes comfortable or stagnant, then what that person will eventually become is a has-been.

What a businessperson must do is search for a strategic positioning by focusing on marketing and customer service. It's one thing to get a customer; it's another thing to keep a customer. Marketing gets the customer, but exceptional customer service is what keeps the customer. So in times like these that are exceptionally competitive, you must find those things that you can do to keep your people satisfied.

I remember reading about a company in a business journal that said it's not our intention to satisfy customers, it's our intention to amaze them. I think that's what people are looking for right now and what they will spend money on. So to escape business failure, one must always be aware of what's happening in the marketplace and how what is happening there will affect customers. Make sure that your marketing and customer service is reflective. There's a distinct difference.

Wright

What is your strategy for achieving financial goals?

Davis

As a seminar leader, I teach a concept that says successful people do what unsuccessful people fail to do. It's a very simple concept but it's true. The same thing applies in the area of finances. What I've done is to pattern myself after some of the top people in the world who have a grip on how wealth is created and how money works. *Forbes* magazine has recently put out a billionaires list, as they do annually. Three of the people on the *Forbes* list I personally know and get informal coaching from. Others on the list whom I don't know or have personal contact with, I still take the time to study and I observe what they do.

What I have found is quite interesting. When I find patterns and strategies that work, I begin sharing it with my clients, friends, and others within my sphere of influence. Since you have a copy of this book, I want you to consider yourself an extension of this special family. The formula involves simply asking and answering a set of questions. The most powerful question you can ask is: what is your highest income-producing activity? People often think in terms of projects and assignments, but they don't think about their highest income-producing activity. This question helps one get the clarity, concentration, and power one needs when fine-tuning his or her financial goal achievement plan.

Now, here are the numbers that go along with this formula. Generally speaking, there are 365 days in the course of a year, so if you take away things like weekends, holidays, vacations, religious observance days, and so forth, what is left is approximately 238 days in which to earn the income you desire. If you multiply these 238 days by an average of 10 working hours per day (entrepreneurs put in a little bit more time than that) you are dealing with approximately 2,380 real work-time hours in the year.

Here's where things get fun. Let's say your goal is to generate $100,000 a year, which means you must be earning $42 per hour. (You arrive at this number by dividing yearly income by total available hours.) If you want to make, let's say, a million dollars a year, then you must be earning $420 per hour. If you want to make $10,000,000 a year, then you must be earning $4,200 per hour. You can use this formula as a focal point to begin looking at your highest income-producing activities and determine that if this is the income you want to earn this year, then you must chose your highest income-producing activities. If you come up short, then you must find another way to make up the difference to support the kind of dollar figure during those available working hours.

Here are the questions you should ask yourself and/or your team to keep you moving in the right direction to make sure that you don't lose insight or focus throughout the course of the year:

1. What activity or activities generate your highest producing income?
2. What are you spending your time doing?
3. Are you focused on the real moneymakers or are you focusing on time-wasters?
4. Are you making it easy for yourself to be a high-income earner or are you doing the things that can be done by someone whose income goal is somewhat less than yours?

In order to earn the income per year that you want, you absolutely must be doing activities every hour that cause your income to line up with this chart. If you catch yourself doing anything that isn't your absolute highest-producing income activity all the time, you are, in effect, making it much harder to achieve your desired financial goals.

This is what I do and have taught my clients for many years. I believe this is one of the great secrets to achieving your financial goals. When you view your time this way, you'll stop doing the insignificant things with your time and you'll begin doing the work that yields the greatest results.

Wright

You talk about "transformational vocabulary." What is it and how can you use it to serve you?

Davis

I define transformational vocabulary as *using the power of words to transform how you feel because how you feel controls, to a large extent, what you do, and what you do affects your results.* We all know the power of words. We've all heard the expression: "sticks and stones may break my bones but words will never hurt me." As we've come to understand, that is simply not true. Words are powerful—they can cut or they can heal. Words play a vital role in shaping our experience of life.

I'm going to give you an example of that. If you take four words that are exactly the same, use them in two different sentences but change it up a little, you'll see what I mean about experience. Here is the example: Teri bit the dog. That's one way. The second way is: The dog bit Teri. Now, they're the exact same words but the experience is considerably different, especially if you're Teri. If you use words in the proper order, they can change your experience. You can instantaneously change how you think, how you feel, and how you live, all by the words you're using. You may be using words like angry/ happy/ excited or nervous/ depressed/ exhausted/ bored. But if you expanded that vocabulary just a little bit, and instead of saying you're angry you could say something like, "I'm disenchanted." Instead of using the word "depressed," you could say, "I'm on the road to a turnaround." Instead of saying you're scared, you could say you're excited or curious. You see the difference? It's all in choosing to use your words wisely.

What I've made a habit of doing is focusing on and using positive, prosperous words because positive, prosperous words lead to prosperous thoughts. Prosperous thoughts lead to prosperous action. Prosperous action moves us to prosperous results. It all begins with our words.

Wright

Do you have any last thoughts that you would like to leave with our readers?

Davis

Yes, I do. The last thing I'd like to say today in my brief time with you is this: With everything that is happening globally today in the economy, in healthcare, in the environment, with human rights, and with our liberties and freedom, we can get so confused, so scattered in our thinking, so fearful and overwhelmed that we lose our way. However, when we say *yes* to life, life itself begins to have an entirely new meaning.

This *Yes You Can!* project will help you work on you so you can see the possibilities in your life and answer *yes* to life when life calls. Believe me, life will call; the question is, will you answer and how will you respond?

Yes Man, a 2008 movie starring Jim Carrey, is an interesting illustration of what I've been talking about. His character, Carl Allen, says yes to just about everything, whereas before, he used to say no to everything. We watched how Allen's life transformed and went from being this *dead,* closed guy emotionally to becoming an *alive,* open guy emotionally.

What all the readers of this interview must understand is that if you're going to say yes to your potential and become the hero in your life, you have to understand that success is in your hands and begins with you saying yes to life's opportunities. Recently I was invited to come to Miami to spend some time with former President Bill Clinton. I had the chance to shadow him for a day. My driver took me to Miami and we arrived in the city. This was a very big moment for me but what I didn't understand was just how big it was.

As I came closer to the neighborhood of the University of Miami I noticed that everything had been locked down—barricades were everywhere. Law enforcement had locked up the city. Without clearance you weren't allowed access. I phoned my contact person in President Clinton's entourage, but for some reason I couldn't get him on the line. It was as though the phone was turned off.

As I sat there wondering what I should do next, I was interrupted by a police officer's tap on my window. The police officer spoke authoritatively. You could feel the testosterone as he asked, "What's your business here?"

"I have an appointment to see the President," I replied.

He looked at me, and said, "Yeah, right." Then he put one hand on his gun.

"No!" I said, "Seriously, I'm here to see the President."

I could see the disbelief in his eyes, but he radioed with one hand on his shoulder radio. His other hand never left his gun. The call went something like this: "I've got this guy named Earl Davis out here and he's saying he's here to see the President. Do you know of any Earl Davis coming today?"

There was a little static on his shoulder radio then all of a sudden you could hear a voice say, "Earl Davis—the Olympic Torchbearer? The success coach? *Yes!* We're expecting him. Don't tell me you've detained him."

Then I could see the embarrassment on the officer's face and said, "Oh ye of little faith, open up the gate, man, and let me through." And he did. It was a really cool, special moment, David.

During my time with President Clinton, he shared a story with me. The story is a very touching one and I believe it is fitting for what we're talking about today.

As the story goes, there was an old man who lived in a tiny village who was known for his wisdom. He had what most people would think is some psychic ability. This man could guess what items were being held without being able to see them.

There were young men in the village who would come and try to trick the man and prove him wrong—that he was a fake and a charlatan. The young men never were successful.

One day, one of the boys had an idea. He thought he would get a little bird and hide it behind his back. He would ask the old man to tell him what was in his hands and whether the item in his hands was dead or alive. So he went before this old man and he asked, "What's in my hand?"

"You have a little bird," he replied.

"Is the bird dead or is it alive?"

The old man sat there for quite a bit and was really quiet. This man knew that if he said the bird was dead that the young man would open his hands to release the bird and let the bird fly away. If he said that the bird was alive, then the young man would crush the bird and kill it.

With his gift of wisdom and perception the man simply said, "The answer lies in your hands."

That's what this *Yes You Can!* project is about today. It's alerting people to the fact that they can realize their "specialness," it's alerting people to the fact that they can reach their potential, it's alerting people to the fact that they can go far beyond anything that they've ever imagined, and that they can achieve their destiny—that it's their moment in time. With this book that you're holding, success lies in your hands. Now, if the economy is great, that will help you, too. If you have support, resources, and money, that will also help. But all those things are *minor* things. The *major* thing is that *it's up to you.*

And that's how I'd like to end our conversation today—it's up to you. I believe that if you say yes to yourself, you'll see a beautiful new world of infinite possibilities open before you.

Wright

What a great conversation, Earl. I really appreciate all the time you've taken with me to talk about some of the most important things we all need to realize and how we all need to act.

Today we've been talking with Earl Davis. Earl is a powerful speaker and success coach. His company, Create Winners, works with corporate professionals, entrepreneurs, small business owners, network marketers, not-for-profits, and individuals who want to bring out the best in themselves and others.

Earl, thank you so much for being with us today on *Yes You Can!*

Davis

I'd like to send the readers of this book off with these words. It's a signature that I'm known by. It doesn't matter whether I'm in the States or abroad. It is very important to remember this in your journey of discovery. It is a poem by Larry S. Chengges:

Follow your dreams wherever they lead,
Don't be distracted by less worthy deeds.
Shelter them. Nourish them. Help them to grow.
Hold your dreams deep, down deep where dreams grow.
Follow your dreams, pursue them with haste,
Life is too precious, too precious to waste.
Be faithful, be loyal in all that you do,
And the dream that you follow will keep coming true.

David, it's been an absolute pleasure and privilege to be with you today.

Earl Davis, Jr., is one of America's most respected voices on human potential and the psychology of winning. Creator and host of the television/radio program *The Winner's Circle*, his clients include Hilton Hotels, IBM, the U.S. Army, statesmen, professional athletes, and entertainers. His company, Create Winners, Inc., works with corporate professionals, entrepreneurs, network marketers, individuals, and people who want to bring out the best in themselves and others.

Earl Davis, Jr.
Create Winners, Inc.
P.O. Box 82006
Tampa, FL 33682
813-672-3445
www.createwinners.org

CHAPTER 11

Obtaining Optimum Energy and Health for Success

by Dr. Richard Bunch

David Wright (Wright)

Maintaining optimal mental acuity and energy in order to think more clearly and to be more creative to see our goals accomplished is one of the biggest keys to achieving success and optimum health today. However, the stress of today's 24/7 society can easily rob us of both physical and mental energy. Our expert to help us understand how to harness energy in our bodies and maximize brain power is Dr. Richard Bunch.

Dr. Bunch attended the prestigious United States Military Academy at West Point in his younger years and later obtained a medical PhD in studies of the brain and nervous system as well as a clinical degree in physical therapy. He is a professional speaker, industry consultant, and owner of physical therapy clinics with a nationwide consulting network.

Dr. Bunch, you are well known for your motivational health lectures worldwide that focus on achieving success in our personal lives and in business by using what you describe as a "no-excuse" self-disciplined approach to mental and physical fitness. In fact, I understand that you feel that the loss of creative energy due to physical and mental fatigue is the single biggest barrier to achieving goals in life and obtaining maximum success in the twenty-first century. I find your opinion that impaired memory with age, which we all complain about so much, has less to do with aging of the brain as it does with how poorly we handle mental stress with age.

Before we go into details of your approach on how to improve our creative and physical energy, would you tell our readers a little more about why and how fatigue is such a big problem today?

Dr. Richard Bunch (Bunch)

Yes, it seems that everyone today is complaining about being overworked and stressed out. Certainly, the stress related to the increased demands of multitasking is a contributing factor to being fatigued. However, if people can better understand how to recognize and manage the sources of their stress, as well as how to improve health, then they are able to focus better on goals and achieve those goals.

One of the problems we must understand is the way the brain is structured. We have a huge number of brain cells called neurons that form a complex network and function like a master computer. The neurons in the outer part of the brain, referred to as the cortex, help us filter out and fine-tune information so that we can focus on ideation and problem-solving. However, whenever we feel overwhelmed, we feel stress. The feeling of stress results in an increased production of neurotransmitters in the brain that causes an over-stimulation of neurons. This over-stimulation leads to the formation of electrical interference patterns. These electrical interference patterns not only make it more difficult to think clearly, but they also lead to accelerated mental fatigue and impaired memory. It is analogous to working with a computer that has a hard drive that is 90 percent full and is operating very sluggishly.

It is not uncommon these days to hear people talk about how their brains are feeling foggy at times and how they cannot really think as sharply as normal. When people find themselves having difficulty with mental focusing, they often feel that it is the result of getting older. But in most cases that is simply not true. There are many older people who think very clearly, very sharply, and who are quick on their feet.

I found from my own personal life, as well as from experiences with thousands of people I have lectured to across the world, that one of the keys to mental clarity and achieving maximum success in life is knowing how to successfully manage stress. This involves taking two major steps:

Step 1: Identify and manage the true sources of stress.
Step 2: Prevent the harmful effects of stress.

When these two methods are truly mastered, people find out quickly that they can tap into a very significant amount of mental and physical energy, think more clearly, and be more creative. After all, being at our best mentally is truly the key to being successful in our personal lives and business.

A huge component of being successful today also relates to *endurance*—both physical and mental endurance. There is a well known saying that "fatigue makes a coward of us all." Most people will agree that this saying is very true. When we feel fatigued, the world looks bleak and our self-confidence plummets. In reality, physical and mental fatigue is intricately interlocked physiologically as components of a vicious cycle. When we feel too tired to do what we have to do, we feel more stress.

My wife, Ellen, who is a registered nurse and president of my company, has often expressed her fear of becoming too tired at times to complete a work project. I can tell when she becomes physically tired that the fear of not being able to complete work she has set out to accomplish for the day becomes a source of major mental stress. As a result, she has learned to avoid this source of stress by getting a good night's sleep and exercising.

I have experienced the same reaction as well and feel that most people do. Unfortunately, when we feel stressed, we do not sleep well, exercise, or eat healthy. This pattern leads to greater physical fatigue and too often, illness. More physical fatigue leads to more mental stress and less quality of sleep. This vicious cycle leads to a compromised immune system and deterioration of our health.

In order to break up this "stress-fatigue" vicious cycle, we need to become more self-disciplined about controlling our lives. Inherent in this process is to embrace an attitude for success and remember that there are no excuses for failure. Each person has within themselves the capacity to achieve personal success when it comes to controlling the lifestyle factors that are largely responsible for the vast majority of health problems and personal failures.

My basic philosophy of self-discipline and accepting that there are no excuses for failure evolved from my days at the United States Military Academy in West Point, New York. As West Point cadets, we were never allowed to give an excuse for our failures. For example, if we failed to meet the time requirement for running a mile while wearing army boots and a fifty-pound backpack, we could not tell our commanding officer that we failed because we didn't get much sleep the previous night. If we did try to render any excuse for failing, we soon found ourselves "walking the yard" for hours on the weekend as punishment. In fact, we were only allowed to respond in one way whenever questioned about a failure and that response was an emphatic "No excuse, sir!" That type of discipline was tough to accept at first. However, West Point taught us that if we make excuses for failing, we choose to take the easy road out, rather than the harder road of pushing ahead and succeeding. We also learned that making excuses for failing could be habitual and a subconscious way to cope with challenges. Discipline was the value taught and success was the reward. Once that "no-excuse" concept took hold of me, I found that I could essentially accomplish anything that I set my mind to do. It was certainly liberating and confidence-building.

So let's begin by looking at the four main lifestyle risk factors that lead to reduced energy and poor health. These are:

1. Stress,
2. Sleep deprivation,
3. Lack of physical exercise, and
4. Poor nutrition.

These four lifestyle risk factors are related to an estimated 90 percent of the medical problems that prematurely age us, disable us, and kill us. They are also linked to reduced cognitive skills, poorer memory, presenile dementia, and Alzheimer's disease. Therefore, in order to achieve optimum health, we must recognize and manage stress, learn how to obtain quality sleep, exercise regularly, and eat healthier.

I know, I know, we all have heard this song and dance before, as we have all talked about reducing stress, getting more sleep, exercising more, and eating healthier; but that's the problem—it's all talk and no action. If we really understood the real value of sleep, exercise, and proper nutrition, we would be much more motivated to do what it takes to become healthy, both mentally and physically. After all, medical research shows that stress, sleep deprivation, lack of exercise, and poor nutrition not only contribute to declining health of our muscles, ligaments, bones, and hearts but also to our brains! So if we can get a handle on all four of these identified lifestyle risk factors that destroy health, we can better position ourselves to achieve maximum energy from good health that is so important for achieving success in our personal lives and business.

Wright

That's fascinating and it sure makes a lot of sense. Stress, inadequate sleep, lack of exercise, and poor nutrition certainly seem to be common problems in today's world, and I can easily see how fatigue results from the modern lifestyle and robs us of our creative juices.

I can also see how a loss of physical and mental energy can adversely affect my career, my marriage, and relationships with friends and family, so what is the first step in your formula for increasing both physical and mental energy that can lead to optimum health, success, and happiness?

Bunch

Well, the first step may sound simple but it's essential to success. Without it, all fitness and diet programs fail. The first step is to consciously make a profound paradigm shift in what I call our priority pyramid. That paradigm shift involves *placing health at the very top of the priority pyramid* over all other obligations.

I can tell you that if you are married, work, and have children, that your entire focus is on work and taking care of your family. Unfortunately, this often occurs at the expense of your health. The average person does not wake up each morning planning his or her day around exercise and proper nutrition. Instead, people typically wake up each day and immediately start a routine centered on work and family demands. We may actually think it is noble to sacrifice health in order to take care of the family and job, but what good are we to our families and employers if we die or become sick and disabled?

I will never forget an event that I experienced years ago when I was consulting on an offshore production platform. After my helicopter had landed, a paramedic met me on the heliport to inform me that a contractor had only moments earlier fallen down dead. He brought me to look at him. I was saddened to find out that the victim was only forty years old. He was obese. I estimated his height at five feet eight inches and his weight at three hundred pounds. I also noted a pack of cigarettes hanging out of his left pocket. I did not have to be a rocket scientist to figure out that this man probably killed himself by a lack of self-discipline, by not taking care of himself.

Not knowing this person personally I found myself looking down at his body and reflecting on the situation. To my surprise I not only felt sadness, but I also felt anger. I felt anger because I realized that his death was premature and so unnecessary. I learned from his friends that he was a hard worker, a good husband, and a wonderful father. But his lack of self-discipline and focus when it came to health robbed his wife of a devoted husband and his two little children of a loving father. It made me realize that when we do not take care of ourselves, we are actually hurting our families and friends even more. After all, this man's suffering was over, but his wife and children, I am sure, are still suffering from his loss today, many years later.

So when we do not take care of ourselves, when we decide to eat whatever we want, as much as we want, smoke, drink excessive amounts of alcohol, avoid exercise, let stress overrun us, and get inadequate sleep, we are actually saying to our families and friends that we do not care enough about them to take care of ourselves. I know people do not consciously think that way but, nevertheless, the behavior has the same effect and outcome.

Having said this I would like to pause here to say emphatically that I am not some type of hard-nosed fitness nut. I do realize there are people reading this who have medical conditions, disabilities, and illnesses that have occurred or developed through absolutely no behavioral fault of their own. These people have my most profound sympathy, prayers, and well wishes. However, after thirty-three years of being in clinical practice, I honestly believe such people represent a relative minority of the cases of people who suffer from bad health, disability, and early death. So please realize that I am addressing only the people who, by their poor lifestyle behaviors and their lack of self-discipline, are killing themselves. For these people it is time to wake up, look in the mirror, and take responsibility for any behaviors that destroy health before it's too late.

So what happens when we truly make that paradigm shift of placing health on the top of life's pyramid of priorities? Well, that should be easy to figure out. When health really becomes our priority in life, depending on our circumstances, we become better spouses, better friends, better parents, better employees, better managers, and better bosses. We will have more mental and physical energy, our immune system will become stronger, we become sick less often or not at all, our personality improves, we think more clearly, we become more creative, and we make better decisions.

What does making the health paradigm shift mean in practical terms? It means that every time we get up in the morning the first thing we do is think about our health and plan how we will eat healthy and exercise today. When this happens, we find that everything else falls in place.

Most accomplished people today will testify that nothing creates the formula for success in life more than a disciplined conviction to achieving personal goals. Failure to take the necessary steps to invest in our most valuable possession—health—is probably the biggest barrier to acquiring success in our business and personal lives. Many companies today are experiencing reduced worker productivity costing billions of dollars annually in the United States due to a phenomenon called "presenteeism." This involves thousands of employees who are physically present at work but are not fully productive because of reduced physical and mental energy related to illness and pain.

Since most people fail in endeavors that lack a conscious conviction to sacrifice and succeed, the paradigm shift to consciously place health on the top of our priority pyramid is critical for succeeding in acquiring optimum health. If we are unable to do that, then nothing else will work. Without such a commitment, we can read all the fitness and diet books we want but nothing will change except that our waistlines will become bigger and our arteries more clogged. The simple fact remains that if we do not have the willpower to truly prioritize health in our lives, we will not succeed in any type of fitness or diet program. We will experience the ultimate failure—we will fail in life.

Wright

You know, you're right. I never wake up in the morning and plan my day around eating healthy and exercise. In fact, I usually wake up fatigued from inadequate or poor quality sleep, and the first thing I think about is all the things that I have to do for my family and my work. Health is something that I think about occasionally but, now that you mention it, and if I'm truthful, it's really not a priority in my life. Making that paradigm shift would be wonderful, so how do I get started?

Bunch

Well, the first thing we do, of course, is make a conscious decision to commit to planning each day around health, 365 days a year. Once we really feel we have made that commitment, then it's time to roll up our shirt sleeves and start working on our plan to achieve optimum health. The next step is to effectively manage stress and get sufficient sleep. This step is critical, will provide us with more energy than we ever imagined, and will make it easier to exercise and eat healthy.

Most people view stress as an abstract psychological sensation. After all, stress is what we perceive it to be. In reality, stress is a psychological phenomenon that creates a very strong physiological response. The physiological reaction to stress is created by the "stress center" located deep in the primitive part of our brain. The stress center functions to prepare our bodies for the "fight or flight" response to a stress reaction. The severity of the "stress reaction" varies among people and occurs in response to events in life that create emotional reactions related to adversity, anxiety, fear, and anger.

Stress is the great robber of our time, of our life. For example, how many times have we driven from work to home and not remembered how we got there? We were on automatic pilot. Why? Our minds were somewhere else. Stress causes us to lose contact with the present and directs our conscious thoughts to something we did yesterday or something we have to do tomorrow. Consequently, life just passes us by.

I'll never forget the time many years ago when I was walking with my young daughter, Leslie, to church on a Sunday morning. My mind had wandered and I was thinking about all the things I had to do at work on Monday. I was not even enjoying the precious time with Leslie. All of a sudden, while walking, Leslie tugged hard on my hand and suddenly brought me back to reality. I looked down and focused on her for the first time that morning. She looked up at me with a big grin and wide eyes and pointed to the sky and said, "Look, Daddy!" I looked up to the sky where she was pointing to see a brilliant, unbelievably beautiful double rainbow. It dawned on me a little later in church that I would have never seen that wonderful event of nature if my daughter had not grabbed my attention. This is just a small example of how easy it is to miss out on beautiful things in life when we are stressed and not living in the present. We inherently know this. One moment we have a baby girl in our hands and the next moment we're walking that baby girl to the wedding altar. Time goes by too quickly. We certainly do not need to accelerate it by letting stress rob us of our time.

The importance of stress management becomes much more important to us when we understand the link between stress and serious illnesses such as heart disease, cancer, and diabetes. The link to these diseases is best understood when you realize what the stress center in the brain is trying to accomplish. When the brain perceives we need to fight or run away from danger, it initiates a series of complex physiological reactions mediated through hormones like cortisol and neurotransmitters like adrenaline. These physiological reactions result in elevating sugar (glucose) and fat in the blood (fuel for muscles so we can fight or flee!).

Stress also increases LDL, the bad cholesterol carrier. LDL is the transporter of cholesterol into our blood vessels. Neurotransmitters produced in response to stress make our muscles tighten up and constrict blood vessels. The combined effects result in elevating our blood pressure. The elevation of stress neurotransmitters also causes our metabolism to speed up, resulting in an accelerated loss of vitamins and minerals from our body that compromises our immune system.

Now, keep in mind that all of these physiological reactions to stress are not bad for us in short-term situations. However, think about the effects of these same physiological reactions when stress is chronic, happening over a period of days, months, and even years in response to modern types of stressors such as divorce, economic hardships, stressful job demands, illnesses, deaths in the family, and so on. The physiological reactions of chronic stress over time have very harmful effects on our health.

We are well aware that our population is becoming fatter. There is a strong link between stress and obesity that must be understood. The hormone insulin is produced by the pancreas in response to elevated blood sugar levels from stress. Insulin's main role in response to stress is to remove excess sugar from your blood. It also converts excess sugar into body fat (namely triglycerides). To make matters worse, while insulin is converting blood sugar to fat, it is also inhibiting hormones that normally help the body burn fat and calories. Thus, excessive production of insulin, a condition known as "hyperinsulinemia," is considered to be one of the underlying physiological reasons that more than two thirds of adults and more than one quarter of children in the United States today are overweight or obese.

The sudden lowering of blood sugar by insulin leads to a condition of hypoglycemia (excessively low blood sugar). This makes us feel very fatigued and interferes with the brain's ability to concentrate. It also creates cravings for more sweets due to the need to elevate the blood sugar level that insulin lowered. It is well known that people under stress commonly eat more sweets. Therefore, we actually eat more to medicate against the effects of stress on our blood sugar levels. It is easy to see how another type of vicious cycle can develop in response to stress in which we suffer from a continual hyperinsulinemia-hypoglycemia cycle.

There is more alarming news about the harmful effects of chronic stress on the brain. Chronic stress has been shown to cause atrophy (or wasting away) of neurons in the deep area of the brain called the hippocampus. This is very relevant as the hippocampus is an important part of the brain for short-term memory, focusing attention, and learning. It is also important to know that sleep deprivation causes many of the same harmful effects to the hippocampus. In fact, the kind of damage to the nervous system caused by chronic stress and sleep deprivation has been correlated to dementia!

Overloading the nervous system from stress, unfortunately, is easier as we become older. This is because as we get older, there are hormonal changes in our bodies that cause stress hormones and neurotransmitters to be elevated in the blood at higher levels in the absence of stress. When stress occurs, the presence of stress hormones and neurotransmitters lasts longer in older people. Also, we suffer from more fractionated sleep as we grow older. So as we age, dealing with stress in the twenty-first century becomes more difficult to handle as our physiological capacities to handle stress and sleep properly decreases.

It is evident that learning how to manage stress and preventing the harmful effects of stress, especially as we age, become very important to our health and success in life. Eliminating or reducing background noise in the brain from stress and improving the quality of sleep by managing stress will make us feel more relaxed and more focused. When we learn how to manage stress, we find that our memory improves and we feel sharper.

Sleep deprivation is a big problem today at all ages. There is a strong relation between sleep disorders and stress. In fact, the best sleeping pill in the world for most people is the absence of stress. How many times have we tossed and turned in bed at night unable to sleep during a work week, but as soon as we go on a vacation we sleep like a rock. The reason for the "vacation effect" on sleep should be obvious. While on vacation we do not worry about e-mails, ringing telephones, project deadlines, or tedious and demanding business meetings. Our minds are more at ease and the excitation of all those extra neurons in our brain from stress does not happen.

So how do we effectively deal with stress? Well, there are two steps to successfully deal with stress. The two steps involve:

1. Recognizing and managing the causes of stress and
2. Preventing the harmful effects of stress we cannot manage effectively from step number one.

The first step—recognizing and managing the causes of stress— requires us to consciously and honestly analyze the real causes of our stress. During this analysis it is helpful to write down the following categories that are common sources of stress today:

> People problems
> Money problems
> Self-image problems
> Attitude problems
> Work-related problems
> Leisure time problems

Under each heading above we should write down the sources of our stress. This requires addressing each of these categories honestly and asking ourselves pointed questions.

In reference to "People Problems," for example, have we had problems or conflicts with a friend, family member, or co-worker? If so, we should write down a plan to resolve the conflict even if it means that we may have to swallow a little pride and take the first step by apologizing.

Regarding "Money Problems," are we spending more than we make? Are we being irresponsible with credit cards? Our plan may be to develop a budget and cut up most of our credit cards.

Likewise, we address all the other topics and develop specific plans to resolve the stressors identified. How do we feel about our jobs? How can we make our jobs better? Are we afraid to say "no" to people? Do we take on more work than we can handle? Do we fail to delegate work when we should? Do we communicate respectfully with co-workers and our bosses? Do we take enough vacation time to relax and decompress? Are we friendly with others and do we try to help others? Do we have any illnesses that we are dealing with? Do we have problems with our self-image? Do we need to exercise and go on a diet? Do we need to make a wardrobe or hairstyle change to improve our self-image?

Whatever the issue may be in our lives, once we honestly identify problems that are causing stress, we need to write down an action plan for resolution and carry the action plan out. The actual act of planning and carrying out the steps of our action plans, even before they are accomplished, will significantly reduce our stress levels. The reason is simple. The stress reduction effect happens when we begin to feel that we are in more control of our lives and we see the proverbial light at the end of the tunnel. For some people, this is a feeling they have not had in a long time. If we follow this simple plan on a regular basis, we will all be amazed at how beneficial it is for lowering stress in our lives.

The second step of dealing with stress is to know how to prevent or at least reduce the harmful effects of stress that will happen no matter what. There is no better way to reduce the harmful effects of stress than by exercising and eating healthy. Exercising has numerous beneficial physiological effects that include the production of neurotransmitters known as endorphins. Endorphins are morphine-like substances produced in the brain that inhibit the harmful effects of stress. Endorphins are produced by aerobic exercise. Unfortunately, people find that eating also causes an increase in the production of endorphins and too often choose to medicate against stress by eating rather than by exercising. Here is where the self-discipline must come into play. Fight stress by exercise and you find health. Fight stress by overeating and you find obesity and disease.

Exercise, in addition to causing an elevation of healthy endorphins, will increase HDL, the good cholesterol carrier. HDL will help offset the effects of increased LDL production that occurs in response to stress. HDL actually carries cholesterol out of blood vessels and brings it to the liver where it is converted into harmless bile. High levels of cholesterol in the blood are a well-known risk factor for cardiovascular disease. Since HDL is elevated mainly by exercise, cardiologists and physical therapists recommend aerobic exercises along with a proper diet to help prevent cardiovascular disease. Removing plaque-causing cholesterol in the arteries in the brain is also an important way to help prevent strokes and poor mental functioning.

Wright

I had no idea how important stress management and sleep was to my health, especially as I get older. Improving clarity of thought, improving memory, creativity, and improving my outlook on life by reducing the interference of stress overload on my brain does make a lot of sense. This is so important today as more and more people are forced to put off retirement due to the economy. They work longer, which has to be stressful to manage.

Based on what you've just described, using these methods I can not only improve my mental processing, creativity, and personality, I can also extend my life and live a better quality of life. The relationship between renewed energy levels and success in my personal life and in business is amazing. You have me hooked, so what else can I do to increase my energy and improve my health?

Bunch

Besides managing stress we need to also *improve our quality of sleep*. Sleep deprivation is a huge problem today and has serious health consequences. Sleep deprivation, like chronic stress, is related to increased risk of cancer, heart disease, and diabetes.

As mentioned earlier, chronic sleep deprivation, just like chronic stress, has been shown to cause atrophy or wasting away of deep parts of our brain that deal with short-term memory, learning, attention, and focus. Therefore, chronic sleep deprivation can adversely affect cognition—the ability to think clearly—and reduce a person's ability to be creative and effectively solve problems. For these reasons it is imperative that we obtain better quality sleep.

So what should we do to help us sleep better? We should avoid habits that make it difficult to fall asleep and stay asleep. Overstimulating the brain from surfing the Web on the computer, eating sweets, and/or drinking coffee late at night should always be avoided. Alcohol may help us fall asleep but it will also cause us to wake up more often, and that translates into poor quality sleep. Therefore, drinking alcohol to fall asleep is not at all advisable.

So what helps us to fall asleep and stay asleep? Simple things such as taking a hot bath and reading a good book before bed will help the brain to relax and make falling asleep easier. Avoid eating late, especially heavy foods, as indigestion can break sleep cycles, not to mention the increased possibility of esophageal reflux that results in burning, acidic fluid entering the throat. Going to bed earlier and getting up earlier in the morning will set patterns for achieving quality sleep.

Research shows that adults need to get at least seven to eight hours of sleep on average. Young children need more sleep time—anywhere from nine to ten hours of sleep. Studies have shown that children who get the recommended amount of sleep regularly perform much better in school than those who do not by retaining information (or learning) easier. Some people may get by with less sleep time depending on the quality of sleep.

The bottom line is that when sleeping we should go through five cycles of sleep several times to benefit from full physical and mental restoration. Sleep cycles one and two represent the light sleep phase. This stage has little, if any, restorative function. Sleep cycles three and four are referred to as "slow wave sleep" and are very important for physical restoration. The fifth cycle of sleep, known as the rapid eye movement (REM) phase of sleep, is essential for mental restoration. We typically dream when we pass through the REM phase. Waking up and feeling refreshed and energetic is the most obvious sign that we have passed through all of these sleep cycles several times and have experienced good quality, restorative sleep. If, on the other hand, we awaken feeling fatigued and experience sleepiness throughout the day, it is likely that we did not achieve good quality sleep.

The next major step to obtaining optimum health in addition to stress management and getting adequate sleep is *exercise*. Most people don't realize that more than two hundred scientific studies have shown that exercise reduces our risks of cancer! These studies show that exercise affects the body at the very molecular level through regulation of DNA, the genetic code that exists in each of our cells and controls cellular function. In simple terms, it is theorized that exercise helps to keep DNA from being damaged and causing our cells to malfunction. Exercise is obviously very important as we age since about three quarters of cancers occur after age fifty-four! This is obviously a big concern to employers and our society, as the current work population is aging.

The American Cancer Association indicates that only about 10 percent of cancers are pre-genetically determined and the remaining 90 percent are related to lifestyles. Remember, the main lifestyle causes of cancer today as determined by research are stress, poor nutrition, and lack of exercise.

Regarding exercise, both aerobics and strengthening exercises are recommended to improve overall health. Of course, we should all get a good examination and clearance from our medical doctor before beginning any exercise program. In general, we should aerobically exercise at least thirty to forty-five minutes a day, every day. That's right, every day! This could simply involve exercise—walking, riding a stationary bicycle or a real bicycle, swimming, or whatever elevates our heart rate and gets the blood pumping. Daily aerobic exercise generates big benefits. It can cut the risk of heart disease and diabetes by my more than 50 percent and reduce the risk of cancer.

Strengthening exercises should also be performed two to three times per week. It is interesting to note that research finds strengthening exercises may even have a greater inhibitory effect on cancer than aerobics! Muscles produce important hormones and chemicals that help regulate DNA that can preserve your health at the molecular level.

So when it comes to exercise, we should be involved in an integrated program involving both aerobic and strengthening exercises. As we age, strengthening to build or tone muscle is probably more important than most of us realize. If we want the fountain of youth, build muscle. I am not talking about taking steroids, of course. I am talking about normal strengthening exercises. In addition, strengthening exercises help protect the joints from being injured, and strong, healthy muscles are our biggest calorie burners. Muscle is critical for maintaining our basal metabolism at an elevated rate so we can burn more calories when inactive. Remember, muscles burn calories while we sleep!

When beginning a strengthening exercise program, it is important to remember to start slowly in order to avoid developing a painful muscle pull or tendonitis. This becomes more likely as we age and lose some of the elasticity of our muscles and tendons. Although I do not recommend intense strengthening exercises for older people, if anyone does become involved in intense strengthening exercises designed to build muscle mass (i.e., to cause muscle hypertrophy), the exercises should not be repeated on the same muscle groups on consecutive days. Skipping a day between heavy strengthening exercises of the same muscle groups is required to allow muscle recovery. Otherwise, serious injury to muscles can occur. However, intense strengthening exercises that rotate to different muscle groups or high rep/low weight strengthening can usually be conducted daily, as long as the daily exercises are not creating any significant pain or prolonged muscle soreness that last more than few hours.

Wright

That's very interesting. I think if more people really understood all the benefits of exercise as you've described it, how to properly exercise, and the underlying changes in the body in response to exercise, they would be much more motivated to exercise. I appreciate you making this so easy to understand.

Now, I assume that since we covered how to increase our energy levels through stress management techniques, improving sleep, and proper exercise, your program also addresses the all-important field of nutrition, right?

Bunch

Of course! Proper nutrition is critical to health. Let's face it, when it comes to eating, the American lifestyle is, for lack of better words, pathological. We eat inadequate breakfasts or skip breakfasts altogether. This results in increasing our hunger by lunchtime. We then overeat for lunch. We also usually eat by convenience—typically very unhealthy processed foods at fast food restaurants. On top of this, we eat unhealthy snacks throughout the day like candy and donuts that add on empty calories and excess weight and make us feel lethargic. We then go home at night and we overeat at dinner. As a consequence, we feel too sluggish and worn out to exercise. So we don't exercise, we watch television (often while snacking), go to bed, and start the day all over again. This is the basic American lifestyle, which is the main reason we are gaining weight like crazy today.

So what to do? When it comes to nutrition I try to keep it simple. Step one for proper nutrition is to start the day off right by eating a good, healthy breakfast (e.g., low fat milk, high fiber cereal, and fresh, raw fruit). When people tell me that they don't like to eat breakfast, I say, you're a grown-up, eat it! No excuse! Skipping breakfast is one of the biggest reasons that we eat too much at lunch. Also, research shows that skipping breakfast elevates cortisol and that adversely affects the regulation of sugar in our blood and causes bouts of hypoglycemia or low blood sugar levels. As with stress-induced hypoglycemia, we feel awful and feel driven to eat more to get rid of the bad feeling that low blood sugar creates. This usually means we eat something sweet or something high glycemic that breaks down into sugar rapidly in order to elevate our blood sugar level. When this happens, insulin—the hormone that controls blood sugar levels—overcompensates and removes sugar rapidly from the blood. As a consequence, we enter into a reactive condition of hypoglycemia. What makes matters worse is that the sugar removed from the blood is converted by insulin into fat called triglycerides. High levels of insulin also prevent fat-burning hormones from working properly. Thus, when we eat high glycemic foods that cause insulin production, we are hit with a double whammy—more fat converted from sugar and less ability to burn fat! Consequently, we gain excess body fat and weight!

Selecting the right food to eat is critical to a healthy diet. Reducing sugar by eating low glycemic foods and avoiding sweets in our diet is an essential step. Reducing sugar in the diet alone works wonders for most people who want to reduce weight. Besides losing weight caused by the conversion of sugar into body fat, we need to understand that sugar is also inflammatory to the body, especially the arteries. This increases the risk for heart disease and strokes. As we know, excess sugar can lead to type II diabetes. In addition, cancer loves sugar! Remember this and you cannot go wrong—excess sugar is toxic to the body.

The problem today is that many people are actually addicted to sugar. Reducing sugar in the diet, therefore, requires a great deal of self-discipline. Most people do not want to stop drinking sugary beverages or reduce their eating of desserts and processed foods. Making a transition from a life-long habit of eating unhealthy high sugary diets to eating healthy is challenging. However, as I have said, there is no excuse for failure. The sacrifice is worth it on so many levels. We need to face the facts. We need to stop the insanity and dump the fast foods and eat more complex carbohydrates such as fruit and vegetables (preferably raw), whole grain breads, and lean meats. Otherwise, we can just wait for the biggest motivator of all—intense fear—the intense fear that no one truly understands until he or she actually has an excruciatingly painful heart attack, becomes paralyzed by a stroke, develops life-changing diabetes, or becomes diagnosed with a life-threatening cancer.

In addition to eating the right kinds of food, we must also eat in a healthy pattern and maintain portion control. The pattern I am making reference to is a pattern of eating that helps us avoid hunger spurts and overeating at major meals. In order to do this we need to eat less food (smaller portions) on a more frequent basis throughout the day that keeps hunger in check. So what is the best pattern for eating healthy and controlling weight? I recommend that we eat six meals a day consisting of:

1. Healthy breakfast
2. Midmorning healthy snack
3. Light lunch
4. Midafternoon healthy snack
5. light dinner
6. Midevening healthy snack

Healthy snacks are not typically found in vending machines, so we must plan in advance to purchase them to bring to work or when we travel. Examples of healthy snacks are raw fruits, vegetables, and nuts (e.g., walnuts, almonds, pecans). These snacks have high levels of fiber and anti-oxidants.

Raw fruit and vegetables also have an additional benefit of offering a natural anti-inflammatory effect on our arteries. Since arteries can become inflamed after eating a meal, especially when eating rich, fatty foods, it is highly recommended that we finish each meal by eating raw fruit and/or vegetables. This dietary habit can potentially prevent a coronary event such as a heart attack. We may also benefit from vitamin and mineral supplements, but it is prudent to check with a medical doctor first. Some supplements may be contraindicated when we are taking certain medications or when we have a medical condition.

While following the six-meal eating pattern, we should also try to avoid sugary beverages and drink more water and unsweetened teas. Again, the overall goal of the six-meal plan is to reduce calories by eating smaller portions and by controlling hunger spurts.

There are so many good diet books on the market, but the one I recommend the most is *The South Beach Diet*.

Wright

Well, Dr. Bunch, your plan certainly makes sense. Would you mind summarizing the key concepts and steps of your approach and describe what would be the best that a person or business could start using today to increase energy, and perhaps achieve higher levels of success in their lives?

Bunch

Yes, I'll be glad to.

Prioritize health. This is the first and the most important step. The key is committing fully to placing health at the top of our priority pyramid and planning each and every day around exercise and proper nutrition. It is easy to say but very difficult to do. It takes discipline and a "no excuse" attitude. Those who do this are the ones everyone wants to emulate.

Reduce the harmful effects of stress. We have to identify the sources of our stress, manage it the best we can, and counter the harmful effects of stress by proper exercise and nutrition. Employers and businesses should also analyze how they increase stress in their employees and learn how to effectively reduce that. They can do this by getting employees more involved in the decision-making process, making their jobs more comfortable (i.e., ergonomics), listening and talking to them respectfully, and not overloading them with work.

Quality sleep. Sleep is essential to physical and mental restoration. Chronic lack of sleep will prematurely age us, compromise our immune system, and lead to deterioration of the parts of our brain that deal with memory and learning. Often, steps we take to reduce stress will also help us obtain better quality sleep.

Exercise regularly. A person should take full responsibility for exercise and employers should encourage exercise among their employees. Businesses should provide health fairs and wellness programs to their employees to promote exercise whenever feasible.

Eat healthy. This means that we have to understand the importance of eating in a pattern not to be hungry and to eat low glycemic foods or foods that break down into sugar more slowly. Complex carbohydrates consisting of raw fruits and vegetables are important components of a healthy diet. Fruits and vegetables also contain many of the vitamins and minerals we need for our immune system, especially as we age. In certain cases, vitamin and mineral supplements may be beneficial and are worthy of consideration. Always check with your medical physician first to see if supplements are right for you.

Finally, allow me to say that I realize that these recommended steps are nothing new. We have heard these recommendations before in one form or the other. Stress management, better sleep, more exercise, and proper nutrition continue to be the issues that research shows to be so important for health. So why do so many of us fail to follow these steps? The answer is simply a lack of discipline and commitment. We have to believe that obtaining optimum health is at the foundation of our personal success and want it bad enough to make the sacrifices that good health requires in today's modern fast-paced society. After all, we not only owe this to ourselves, but we also owe such a commitment to the ones who love us most—our family and friends. We all should live a long, prosperous, and full life and that is my hope and wish for all who read this chapter!

Wright

Well, what a great conversation. I really appreciate all this time you've taken with me to answer these questions. I have really learned a lot and I am sure that our readers will, too.

Bunch

Thank you for having me; I appreciate it.

Wright

Today we've been talking with Dr. Richard Bunch. Dr. Bunch is a professional speaker, an industry consultant, and owner of multiple physical therapy clinics with a nationwide consulting network. Today we've been talking about the energy of success—harnessing energy and brainpower for maximum success in life and business. I don't know about you, but I'm going to listen to Dr. Bunch; he sounds like he knows what he's talking about.

Dr. Bunch, thank you so much for being with us today on *Yes You Can!*

Bunch

Thank you.

Richard Bunch, PhD, PT, CBES, is a licensed physical therapist with a PhD in Human Neuroanatomy and Physiology. He is also an ergonomic specialist and professional speaker who has lectured to hundreds of thousands of people throughout the United States, Europe, Asia, and Africa. He consults with and lectures to industries and conducts seminars and keynote lectures for various national safety and medical conferences.

Dr. Bunch specializes in the integrative proactive approach to preventing lifestyle and work-related injuries and illnesses. He attended West Point United States Military Academy in New York and Louisiana State University Medical Center where he received his clinical degree in Physical Therapy and doctorate (PhD) with honors. He is currently the founder, owner, and CEO of Industrial Safety & Rehabilitation (ISR) Institute based in New Orleans, Louisiana, with a national network of clinics providing proprietary employee functional testing services, behavioral-based injury prevention, and ergonomics consulting and training. He also currently serves as a Clinical Associate Professor at Tulane University Medical Center, Department of Health Sciences.

Richard Bunch, PhD, PT, CBES

ISR Institute, Inc.
1516 River Oaks Road West
New Orleans, LA 70123
985-791-4904
Bunchisr@AOL.com
www.ISR-Institute.com

CHAPTER 12

Generati: The Art and Science of Sustainable Leadership

by Mike Jay

THE INTERVIEW

David Wright (Wright)

Today we're talking with Mike Jay. Mike coined the word "generati" to capture the art and science of sustainable leadership. This generativity concept of leadership helps managers answer key questions about the "who, what, when, where, why, and how" of "being, doing, having, and becoming" every day. I'm talking with Mike about what it takes to be a generative managerial leader in the rising uncertainty of twenty-first century complexity.

Mike, welcome to *Yes You Can!*

Mike Jay (Jay)

Thanks, David. It's great to be a part of this project with you.

Wright

How do we begin to understand what it means to be a "generative managerial leader"?

Jay

I think it will be helpful if I start by describing the leadership terrain that generati addresses. We all pay lip service to the radical acceleration of change in all areas of technology, but yet we often lose sight of its ongoing intensification and the fierceness of its effects and challenges.

Many of us remember our first reading of Alvin Toffler's book, *Future Shock*. He gives the example of the curve of improvements in the speed of transportation and the shortening of the time periods between them. First, there was the camel caravan around 6000 BC at eight miles per hour. Then, around 1600 BC, the chariot came along and could go twenty miles per hour. Cultures had plenty of time to assimilate the effects of the chariot and return to a steady state, because it took about thirty-five hundred years for the steam locomotive to reach one hundred miles per hour, in the 1880s AD. But this time, there was not a long period for society to assimilate the increase and return to a steady state because only a century later, the increase of speed traced an accelerating curve with human beings orbiting Earth in a space capsule at eighteen thousand miles per hour.

Now this was the goal of the founders of our science. Francis Bacon urged us to gain power over nature to improve our lot; Descartes urged us to become masters and possessors of nature. But here's the kicker—it's the success of their grand vision that fostered an ever-increasing acceleration of change that has created the terrain for the new leadership. That acceleration is now creating change in such short periods of time and of such magnitude, diversity, and complexity that it's overwhelming our ability to predict and plan on the basis of knowing. Leaders must now deal with future shock on steroids.

So how can we cope with these conditions of complexity and necessary *un*knowing in a successful way? That's what generati is designed to help us achieve.

Wright

You've been known to introduce this idea of generative leadership by asking the tongue twister of a question: "How will who lead whom to do what, when, where, and why?" Would you answer that for our readers?

Jay

Well, let's begin that by trying to help readers find their place in the framework of this language. This concept of generati and generativity on the part of managerial leaders may sound paradoxical, as if I'm telling them to be less like leaders. The reason is that we're entering a new and most difficult leadership environment, and this is going to call for a somewhat different paradigm of the great leader. I haven't fully introduced this concept before, although it's been emerging from my work over the last twenty-two years. I've kept thinking it can't be this simple. What I've found in testing it over time is that it *is* relatively simple. But it's not easy.

Wright

So let's unpack this starting with the "who" and "whom." Who do you think needs to be the generative leaders in the twenty-first century and who are the followers? Is it just in the business and professional worlds where generative leadership is needed or are there other arenas where it also applies?

Jay

That's a great question to start with because it takes us to one of the major differences between the two leadership paradigms. It is this radical acceleration of change that is forcing a revised leadership model upon us. When things were less complex and change was less constant, we used to be able to designate a leader, assume he or she could know enough to make the guiding decisions, and everyone else became a follower. Now we're *all* going to have to perform leadership functions. The message of this book is, "yes, you can." This begs the question, who is "you"? Is it the individual or the collective you? In what arenas will generative leadership be necessary for success—in the business and professional worlds, or the world of individuals in their normal, everyday lives? As the old joke says, "The answer is yes." Leadership is going to have to come from everywhere.

Wright

Well, let's finish setting the stage by asking the question of "why?" I guess what I'm really asking is "why now?"

Jay

Let's go back to the differences between the old and new leadership contexts. In the old context, to put the matter more simply than it ever actually was in practice, leadership emerged because we had a clear problem and it was stated in a clear context. The leader made a decision, people followed, and that was the way the problem was taken care of. Some leaders were better than others, some problems were harder to come to grips with than others, some crises were unforeseen, and some outcomes created destruction of large population groups, but none of these "problems" were big enough or difficult enough to change the basic model.

Today, with twenty-first century complexity and the acceleration of fundamental changes, plus the expectation that these will continue to grow exponentially, it appears that we are confronted with more than a mere difference of degree in the problems for leadership. We're confronting a difference in kind. The magnitude of uncertainty and the potential impact, in particular, of our outcomes have crossed a line. *The only thing certain is that, more and more, nobody knows or can know what's coming next and that's a different kind of paradigm to operate in.* So how does the leadership appropriate in this context emerge? What must be different in the new leadership that enables it to sustain not only itself, but also human well-being?

Wright

So is generative leadership the domain of a talented few or are there skills and competencies that can be nurtured and developed?

Jay

Well, let's look first at some indicators of generative leadership. Such leadership has to take a certain array of resources and be able to facilitate a direction and goal for people to follow. It has to be able to frame its immediate solution in such a way that it doesn't cause more problems than it solves or use up more resources down the line. And more generally, it has to prevent further negative outcomes. In this leadership terrain we can't think only about growth. Growth and capitalism have been wonderful vehicles to give people who never before had them chances to become a part of mainstream society in all countries. Yet the resource commitment to do that is becoming so high, we need to find a different source of sustainability.

When that subject comes up, most leaders haven't thought through how to unpack it. I've come to unpack it two ways. Given that now we don't know what we don't know, we need to become personally, organizationally, and socially resilient. In other words, we need to design and build structures and practices that allow us to bounce back efficiently, effectively, and sustainably when we meet an unanticipated problem. And we have to become generative. This means being prepared in our structures and practices to generate resources that will carry us forward when we don't have access to all the usual resources.

Wright

So how might these two competencies—resilience and generativity— play out in today's complex business environment? Will you give me an example from the business world you move in as a coach?

Jay

Well, here's an example of one type of problem. I come back to the difficulty of knowing, in such rapidly changing conditions, what long-term investments I need to make in my organization. If you are an airline executive right now, how in the world would you know how much to charge for fuel in three years? There isn't even a border where one side is all old leadership terrain and the other all new leadership terrain. In most cases, the demands are mixed together in complex and sometimes invisible ways. There are times, as a problem emerges, when you can look at what earlier leaders have done and project that forward as a model. But this can be misleading if the context has changed. And here are just a few other factors that feed the fallibility of prediction: Digital technology has increased the speed and reach of communications. No one can hide from what is happening elsewhere in the world. With so many people connected so quickly, global cultural links and social patterns form and dissolve in the blink of an eye, and this happens in unpredictable ways that are both stabilizing and destabilizing. Information technology increasingly updates and makes obsolete what we think we know (the unknown can come disguised as the known). Not knowing is the key problem we are facing as business leaders, professional leaders, CEOs, or political leaders at this juncture in history.

Here is the question I've worked to answer over a long period of time: what can you do if you get into an unforeseen set of circumstances that are also unclear and turbulent? You think you know where you're going and bang! Just when you get everything moving in that direction, the winds change and you're forced in another direction. You can't change this growing tsunami of complexity, but you can alter the way you, your business, your professional practice, your area of political responsibility, even your family *interface with it*. I've built a conceptual toolkit that includes best practices to help anyone work in a sustainable frame of leadership and learn how to generate the resources he or she needs. If you as a leader are going to emerge, or I'm going to coach you to develop resilience and generativity, what is it you've got to have in your toolkit? I've come to think of these "tools" as five meta-competencies: attention, intention, alignment, capability, and coaching.

Wright

So how do these five competencies fit into the resilience-plus-generativity equation?

Jay

We've got a couple of sets of factors moving in the conversation now. Let me give an example of the generative and resilient use of the meta-competency of "attention" and then relate it to "when" in our question that defines the profile of a leadership situation. There's a certain thread in popular ideas about leadership that writes off the most important use of attention. It's captured in the saying, "There's no 'I' in 'team.'" (That's a pun, folks.) The only vowels in "team" are "e" and "a." But it also means to say that for any collaborative project to work, you have to drop the "I" for the good of the project as a whole. Well, there *is* an "I" in "generative team" and more than one "I" in "resilient team." A generative and resilient organization, including its named leaders and everyone who shares leadership functions in the new leadership terrain, must be composed of well-developed "I"s. This is the powerful instrument that a generative team and a resilient team bring to produce the most effective, efficient, and sustainable collaboration.

Generative and resilient leaders, while giving all necessary attention to the task at hand, simultaneously keep their attentive awareness on their own processes of thinking, feeling, and acting. They spontaneously monitor how they are handling the practices and conditions that allow them to do their job and model generative leadership for others. If I'm going to develop resilience and generativity, I have to take care of myself in order to take care of what is happening around me. Can I take care of my information? Can I keep my energy up and the energy of others up? Do I know how to message what it is I'm doing so others can recognize a teachable point of view in it? Do others see me taking responsibility for how I act? This being, having, doing, and becoming of the "I" is the first thing we have to pay attention to and take care of, because insofar as any of us are leaders, everybody is looking to us for cues. We need to model how to be generative and resilient when people look to us in these circumstances of pervasive and highly consequential uncertainty. The very first part of generati is accepting the responsibility for our "I" and taking care of it and, in this context, the "when" is always now. The right "when" emerges from the product of all the factors that the designed allocation of attention delivers to us and how they bear on our relation to our tasks and the well-being and effectiveness of the people around us.

Let me just briefly add that in terms of the meta-competencies, this attention is guided by our intention and in turn guides our ongoing adjustment of our intention as our work unfolds. They are intimately intertwined and inform each other.

Wright

So now we've got the "when." How about the "where"?

Jay

We said that the "when" depends on the context of the unfolding project and setting, and because change is so rapid, we frequently can't predict the "when" with reliability before it emerges. The same thing is true of the "where"—the end state we want to reach through the project, the realized goal. The "where" is defined for us as leaders within a multi-factored context of linked short-term and long-term goals. But here's the question: how do you define, move toward, and achieve, let's say, a desired ten-year goal if you can't predict the major part of the context at five years out, to say nothing of eight years out, and ten years seems a different world if your only certainty is a collection of uncertainties?

Let's look first at the old leadership terrain and contrast it with the emerging new terrain. When there is a relatively clear and gradual shifting of the environment, anyone can put a stake out there and say, "Go from here to there," with perhaps small course corrections as circumstances change. But in the new terrain of endlessly accelerating complexity and change, we can't put a stake in the ground, look at it over a period of time, and have it stay there. For that, we'd have to be able to define the shape of the "where," even though the context that will require it doesn't yet exist and keeps changing unpredictably. It may also turn out to be unnecessary despite the sunk costs and the R and D and production hours. Leading will be more like driving a car toward an intended destination blindfolded, because where the destination is and the way to reach it is constantly shifting in unpredictable ways. You can't simply map and prepare for it.

So what *can* you do? Well, as I put it before, if you can't run faster than the tsunami of complexity and novelty, you can change the way you prepare to *interface with the certainty of uncertainty*. You can understand what your tools are, including your unique character, natural motivations, and talents. More fully, you can know what your personal and organizational identity is and how that identity is manifesting intention through a purpose. The "where" is not yet fully knowable in the sense of possessing a particular form. It is a *potentiality* that exists within you. It is part of your strategic intention—your compass direction that is in some respects provisional. It is captured in the ways you measure how fast you are approaching the realized "where"; how you accelerate or decelerate or shift direction, depending on changing contexts; how you operate in terms of purpose, though the form of its eventual realization may be different than the form you anticipated.

So far I've been speaking of the "where" metaphorically as the end state that manifests our intention and realizes our purposes. I should also mention a *geographical* shift of "where" that introduces a new context affecting the realization of our intentions and purposes. In a world that is shifting its polarity clearly now toward Asia and away from the West, you're going to start to see "where" change dramatically in every sense. How will we change ourselves *here* for a market that is *there*? What will this mean to the complexity of our context? To return to the metaphorical use, how will we be sustainable while using fewer resources and at the same time reach an effective and efficient "where" whose character no one can fully predict?

Wright

So I'm guessing the "how" is the piece that ties all this together?

Jay

The "how" is closely related to a third meta-competency, "alignment." Three questions are key to judging alignment: "What does this project *require* for successful completion?" "What is our available *capability*?" and "How can we *close any gap* between these two factors?" These questions are scalable. You can ask them of an individual or organizational project, of a local or multinational project. Insofar as you know the requirements, know the available capability, and know what is necessary to close the gap between them, then you know the "how." But, we now must follow this pattern, as we have for each of the elements we've discussed, in the framework of accelerating complexity, change, and uncertainty. So we must guesstimate our requirements for the time being and assess our available capability in awareness and that some of its elements may emerge as incomplete or irrelevant as we move ahead. We also have to be very flexible and at times innovative about how we close the gap between requirements and capability. This area, too, surfaces the question, "What does a leader have to do to practice and model sustainable, resilient, and generative leadership to bring together the people who are looking for leadership and to understand how to get into and stay in alignment?"

There's a competitive game or sport some readers may be familiar with called "orienteering." I think it's a remarkably apt workshop exercise to give people a sense of understanding of what it's like to function in the kind of environment I've been describing. The participants can be individuals or longstanding or newly constituted teams. As they start, those participating as individuals, or the leaders in the case of teams, are given a compass. Both at the beginning and along the course, participants are given enigmatic clues that take them through one stage to the next clue and next stage. Some participants may have a gift for decoding these, while those who don't have to find other ways to advance themselves or their teams. All the participants head out with a compass. They don't know where they're going, but can look at the compass and see their direction and know what the compass heading was and know what they're finding along the way. To me, the leader who is sustainable and resilient and generative is going to have to have a good compass and look at the stars, look at the landmarks, look at what's around, and get information from a lot of people to understand how to get to the end of the course. Someone knowledgeable has to set out the course and clues with an eye to what you know about the participants. When it's done as an exercise, the debriefing can be illuminating for everybody.

Wright

Last we have the "what." What does generative leadership all add up to?

Jay

Let me start with a few words about the process called "emergence." In emergent systems, the thing that arises from the original parts can have properties that are different from the properties of the parts. For example, people bake cakes every day. They take specific amounts of flour, eggs, yeast, spices, and some kind of liquid, mix these ingredients together, and place the mixture in an environment that will expose it to a certain degree of heat for a specified length of time. At the end of the process, they remove the mixture from the heat. What emerges has a texture, fragrance, taste, and often a color different from any of the separate ingredients.

Emergent properties are often nonlinear, that is, there's not always a straightforward cause-and-effect relationship between the actions a leader takes, the resources the leader uses, and what happens to the mix over time. Sure, in short periods there may be, but short periods aren't the key framework. The key is how I make long-term investments in leadership, allocate resources that are scarce and expensive, and set prices looking ahead.

Earlier, I talked about the relationship between the requirements of a job and the capability of the individual or organization to do that job; and in any areas where the capability doesn't match requirements, the need to find a way to close the gap between them. In my resilience and generativity training, one way we teach how to close the gap is called "scaffolding." When you look at a building that is being built or a process that is being constructed, one of the most important pieces is not the structure itself, it's the scaffolding. A primary function of leadership for emergence is to create the structures and conditions for positive emergence to occur.

Perhaps I should say here that even with the fundamental focus on emergence, organizations will continue at some levels to have low-level management and support functions that will most effectively be handled when carried out by standard templates for intended results. But high-level leadership will increasingly have to be the kind I've been describing because of the degree of complexity and increasing rate of change in our global environment. These circumstances will force us to choose between adaptation and dissolution. Of course, people working at any level will have greater well-being and productivity with resilience and generativity training.

When you try to answer these questions—How in the world can we think about things that nobody knows how to think about yet? How can we plan for things when nobody knows what is certain?—you approximate what is happening for leaders as we go forward more deeply into uncertainty and turbulence. If you really grasp this, it will make you very uncomfortable. It's this discomfort that compels you to ask: If I don't have enough resources to do the job, how do I generate them? How do I develop resources to handle such unpredictable circumstances? These are really questions about how individuals and organizations shape structures and processes that support emergent solutions. The answer is not to do what we spontaneously do when we are scared by some uncertainty, which is exert top-down, rigid control over the search for security, although there might be a temporary place for that. Long-term, emergent solutions come from collaborations, from conversations, from people with certain types of temperaments and backgrounds. They come from innovation. They come from people who are giving us feedback. They're even going to come from ideas we didn't think would work. They may come in part from autonomous machine intelligence. To return to my earlier metaphor, they're going to come from people working together with somebody bringing the eggs, somebody else bringing some flour, somebody else bringing sugar, and somebody else bringing milk. We're putting all that together and we're all baking a cake together. We won't know how it's going to taste as we would have with an old, familiar recipe. But at the same time, we're going to have to live with the cake. That's not an easy environment.

When you look at leadership and you look at "yes, you can," you begin to see that the present concept of leadership is going to have to shift. We're going to have to start looking at the process of molding it all together so that we can stay resilient no matter what happens and so we can generate enough resources to get the job done. Putting this kind of scaffolding in place is what is needed in generative leadership.

Wright

So is it possible to weave all these threads together into what you might say is a generative fabric?

Jay

Yes. I will soon be publishing a brief, practice-oriented toolkit titled, *Flawless Living Handbook*. It will be followed by my more comprehensive book, *Flawless Living*. These books are designed to weave these threads together into a generative fabric. For our purposes here, I'm going to focus on the subjective threads in the fabric—*the ways you prepare yourself to interface with uncertainty.* So let me briefly come back to this toolkit I mentioned—the set of practices designed to help people learn key elements of sustainable, resilient, and generative formal leadership and informal leadership, which is increasingly important in the conditions of complexity. In terms of the meta-competencies that we've been following through this conversation, the *Handbook* spends substantial time in the early chapters helping you define the precise shape of your identity and capabilities and how you use them to move through complexity and uncertainty with greater well-being.

What is your identity? What are you good at and poor at? What would you do even if you weren't paid to do it? Do you understand how you attribute meaning to everyday events, how your thinking functions, and what motivates and de-motivates you? Do you understand your own developmental trajectory? And do you understand these same factors in the people you work with and live with and that their differences may be in strengths that complement your natural capability? Can you reach out and ask for help from those who have capabilities you do not have? What is your intention moving forward? Do you have gauges you're looking at to monitor your movement? Can you inform yourself, regulate yourself, and remain transparent to your awareness?

When you develop such self-knowledge and the accompanying skills, you will be able to integrate greater well-being into your life despite this increasing complexity and uncertainty. The *Flawless Living Handbook* provides a firm foundation for acquiring the knowledge and skills necessary to live *your* life.

Wright

So in wrapping up, how does a person get started in developing and employing generative leadership?

Jay

There are things you can do, but to do them successfully requires that you keep in your mind the differences between what I've called the old and new leadership terrains. In the older terrain, the relation of input and outcome was somewhat simpler. It followed the law of cause and effect; and causes and effects were slower, more stable, and in most cases more certain. In the new terrain, change and complexity are accelerating so fast that you no longer have the previously reasonable expectation that what you start will have the same relevance down the road as when you started it. If you have the same expectations you had of the older leadership terrain, when you mapped out a goal and pushed it through step after step over time to a prescribed result, what will happen? Now, more and more, new circumstances, resources, or processes will emerge and the original plan won't work out.

What's happening to us now is that it's just overwhelming because it's so easy to fall victim to the old paradigm where you thought that something was certain. Then you come to find out that those assumptions were flawed in this new world where everything is shifting under your feet. By not facing the emerging uncertainty and figuring out how to make some provision for it, *we* victimize *ourselves*. Avoiding this requires that you learn how to manage your own ego. Here we return to a question we treated in a different context earlier—the saying that there's no "I" in "team." There is an "I" in "team" and even more in "leader," but it's an enlightened "I" that is sensitive to the new circumstances.

Even as much as we want leaders who are confident and decisive, we also want people who can manage in this ambiguous environment. You're not going to be able to do that alone because your own view of reality is so small in comparison to the totality of what we're facing amid this uncertainty. So people are going to have to go after their own leadership ego—the one that asks what's in this for me?—and consider whether that precludes what's in it for everybody else. Am I egotistical enough to think that I know what's happening when, in fact, I could not possibly know? This facing up—this staring into the abyss and having nothing stare back—is something that I think is going to scare the hell out of a lot of people. That's why we're seeing more than half of the global 2000 companies shake out about every other year. That's the average right now.

I think one of the easiest steps to get started is to break down the meta-competencies—again, the five meta-competencies I've identified are attention, intention, capability, alignment, and coaching—into their component parts. In other words, there are things we can teach people and that you can learn that allow you to be more resilient and generative in an environment where nobody knows enough to be certain. So how do you get started?

You know, there was a book by Marshall Goldsmith called *What Got You Here Won't Get You There*. It's the same kind of idea here. You may have spent a lot of your life getting to the point of being in a leadership position with a lot of people having confidence in you, only to find out that the acceleration of complexity, change, and uncertainty puts you in what seems an impossible situation.

How do you continue to lead? Well, the first thing is to admit that you don't know. The second thing is to begin to test all of your previous assumptions about reality. Then you need to make sure that you don't get CEO's disease, where people tell you what you want to hear instead of telling you the truth. You have to *believe* that you don't know and because you don't know, you're going to ask other people to help you.

In that regard, here's a takeaway about resilience: as uncertainty increases, the need for resilience increases. Well, then, how do you become more resilient? Research has shown that the number one key is the ability to reach out. Not only do you have to reach out, you have to reach back into yourself and understand clearly who you are, what your capability is, and where you'd better ask for help. It means understanding how you need to ask for help because you have a good relationship with who you are.

So to get back to one of your first questions, to a significant degree anybody can learn to become a generative leader. You do that and become more resilient by getting a handle on what you don't know, by becoming humble in terms of your own ego, and by reaching out to others for the testing of what is real. This sequence is the key, in my view. It's the first step toward generative leadership.

Wright

What an interesting conversation, Mike. You've given me a lot to think about, but I have to admit that you've got it in a logical order so I could follow it. Hopefully I can take these notes and really get into the substance of what you're talking about. It's been very, very interesting and I know our readers are going to get a lot out of it.

Jay

Well, thank you, David. I've never talked about this particular model so fully before. That's why I wanted to be a part of this project—to put a stake in the ground that is moving beneath our feet, not in the hope of establishing a stable target, but to say, look, there is something to be said about leadership yesterday and today.

But there is also something to say about leadership tomorrow because it might not be the same. If we're going to start a dialogue on leadership, then let's start it with the understanding that leadership in our new circumstances has to be generative and has to be resilient in the ways, and for the reasons, I've spoken of here. That's the dialogue I think we need to start in terms of *Yes You Can!*

Wright

Today I have been talking with Mike Jay about what it takes to be a generative managerial leader in the rising uncertainty of our times. Mike has coined the term "generati" to capture the art and science of sustainable leadership.

Mike, thank you very much for being with us today on *Yes You Can!*

Jay

Thanks, David.

 Mike Jay is a professional business coach, consultant, and *happeneur*. An award-winning United States Marine and collegiate athlete, he initially parlayed his leadership experience into agribusiness innovation and management success in medicine, hospitality, and business services. In 1999, he founded a world-class business and executive coach training system. Through more than ten thousand hours of coaching sessions, Mike has served business leaders in twenty-seven countries. He is consistently on the leading edge of leadership innovation, culture change, and *emergenics*—a field he created to explore the nature of creating fewer problems than you solve. Mike coined the term *generati* and has dedicated his life to generative leadership.

Mike R. Jay

1132 13th Ave
Mitchell, NE 69357
877-901-Coach (2622)
www.mikejay.com

CHAPTER 13

Yes You Can Start Over

by Lyn Jeffress

David Wright (Wright)

Today we're talking with Lyn Jeffress. Lyn is Founder and President of Imagined Future Inc., a coaching, consulting, and training organization. Her passion is helping others discover and release their potential and live the life they've only dreamed of. Lyn holds both a master's degree in Leadership and an MBA. In addition, she received her coaching certification from The Hudson Institute and has had the honor of studying with visionary thinkers such as Martin Seligman, Stephen R. Covey, David L. Cooperider, as well as movie producer Stephen Simon.

Through the work of Imagined Future Inc., Lyn helps individuals, teams, and organizations discover and maximize their performance. Her work with teams results in increased understanding of the potential of each member. She also helps to shift paradigms within organizations in order to improve the contribution of each team to the organization.

Lyn Jeffress, welcome to *Yes You Can!*

Lyn Jeffress (Jeffress)

Thank you David.

Wright

So you have been successful in helping individuals discover and launch their potential, how are people responding during these difficult times?

Jeffress

David, what I'm hearing from many of my clients these days is they no longer feel like they're in the driver's seat. Many were caught off guard by changes that have occurred in their lives. What's worse is that they're finding that old processes, methods, and solutions they've used in the past don't seem to be working today. As you noted, these are turbulent times and people are finding that they can no longer count on things they've become accustomed to. Many are fearful, angry, or even feeling paralyzed as they try to deal with the changes imposed on them. And quite frankly, people are feeling that they are not in control.

As you mentioned, my company has been successful in helping people and teams discover and launch their full potential. However, when people begin to give up or feel out of control of their destiny the task of launching that potential becomes ever more challenging.

Wright

Do you think this experience is unique to our economic crisis?

Jeffress

No, David, I don't. What's currently happening in our economy stands out to a lot of people. However, any kind of major change or upset will result in similar feelings, whether that is the result of a job loss, a career change, a failed marriage or relationship, the stereotypical empty nest experience, or being uprooted to a new community, these feelings are not unusual.

In the late 1960s, Elizabeth Kübler-Ross described five stages of grieving and loss. For our readers who may not be familiar with this work, the five stages are: Denial, Anger, Bargaining, Depression, and then, Acceptance. Although the work of Kübler-Ross was specifically focused on terminal illness, what we've come to learn is that those same stages occur whenever a loss is *really significant*. I am seeing this with my clients who have been adversely affected by corporate downsizing and reorganizations.

The amount of time it takes for someone to start anew is directly related to the speed with which they work through the stages. Moving through each stage is not easy. Additionally, people do not work through the stages in a linear fashion. Some individuals may find themselves dropping back into a previous stage as a result of some unanticipated trigger. For example, one client believed himself to be in the "Anger" stage, but our work together revealed the amount of "Bargaining" that he was doing with his former employer as a result of the "Denial" he felt about his job loss. As we examined his denial, we uncovered the triggers for anger.

After working through his anger, we were able to evaluate what, if any, bargaining or negotiating he wanted to tackle with his former employer in order to secure assistance in letting go and finding new work.

The next stage he experienced, that of depression, was short lived as a result of having cleared the previous stages. As new opportunities and ideas presented themselves, he had a much easier time accepting the positive effect of the change against which he had fought so hard.

Wright

Why do you think it's not easy to move on?

Jeffress

What I have found is that we become very attached to things and find it hard to let go of our attachments. Our culture, here in the United States, reinforces attachment to our roles in life or work. When someone asks us, "What do you do?" our response is to provide our personal "label." In other words, we will respond by saying, "I'm a director [teacher, mom, dad, student, or owner]." As you can imagine, once we lose the label, we lose our self-definition. That is especially true in this current economy where a person may have been carrying around his or her label for ten, fifteen, or twenty years. Now, the answer to the question, "What do you do?" is not as easy to answer. Some of the work we've been doing with our clients is to help redefine the essence and potential of the person—not just a label, but a clear picture of who the person is.

David, I'll give you an example of what I'm saying. A few years ago, a close friend of mine traveled to Europe with his family. In meeting another traveling family, the conversation starter for my friend was to ask the other father, "So, what do you do?" To his surprise, the answer went something like this, "Well, we love to travel and see the countryside. We ski and we hike and we do a lot of family-oriented activities. We enjoy eating out as well as cooking together in our home—" and, on and on he went with his answer. This really caught my friend by surprise. His intention for the question—and the answer he anticipated—was to learn the type of work being done by the other father. For my friend, this experience drove home our nature of defining ourselves by what we do, not by who we are or what values we hold.

So, David, there is a point to my story. In our culture, because we have a tendency to define ourselves with a label, a major change in our lives may result in the inability to define ourselves to others, and we can feel *lost!*

Wright

So where would one begin?

Jeffress

Well, I think we must begin by asking ourselves, "What am I attached to?" and "Where are my patterns of attachment?"

Quite honestly, I recommend that individuals seek the assistance of a trained, professional coach or counselor in this initial stage. The attachments we have formed are often very deep and we've become unaware of their power over us. If the expense of working with a professional is currently a challenge, at a minimum, I advise our readers that it is essential to find someone who can be objective in talking with you—someone who can "hold up the mirror" for you to see how you currently define yourself. It is through examination of those patterns of attachments that we will begin to take back control of our own lives.

Wright

So that begs the question, how does the person break the pattern of attachment?

Jeffress

Yes, David, I find that to be an important question. In order to break the pattern, we must first know that it exists and what that pattern has come to mean to us. Once we recognize the patterns of attachment, we can begin to evaluate what the loss—or change--of those attachments represents to us.

- *What do I believe about the change I'm faced with?* When we are faced with significant change, it is not uncommon to think of that change as a loss. As a result of experiencing change as loss, the first thing we tend to ask ourselves is, "What am I going to have to give up in order to get through this situation or through this change?"

I find the easiest way to break the pattern of attachment is to turn that coin over and ask ourselves the following question:

- *In the life that I have been living, what have I been sacrificing in order to hang on to my attachments?* Pondering this question is often a major wake up call. I would advise our readers to begin to answer these types of questions for themselves:

  What's not happening in your life that you wish was a part of it?

  Where do you find that you do not have enough time? And, for whom?

  How is your health?

  How well are you sleeping?

  How strong are your relationships?

  How often do you feel that you are truly having fun?

Wright

Sounds to me as if I started asking myself those kinds of questions it would certainly bring up new priorities, right?

Jeffress

That is it exactly, David. The goal of this exercise is to change your perspective. By looking at your change through the lens of what might be currently missing, not what you're giving up but what are you missing out on, you give yourself something new upon which to focus. If the attachments you've developed have caused you to set aside other priorities. The time of change is the perfect opportunity to re-evaluate your life and your priorities. When you look at what you miss, or what you are not spending time on, you can begin to see a new way of living your life. This allows you to begin moving forward.

First, you've explored your patterns of attachments. Second, you've evaluated other priorities that you may have put on the back burner.

The next question to ponder is, "What did I want to accomplish in my lifetime?" Asking yourself this question will also help you identify dreams that you have set aside.

Wright

So what would be the next step?

Jeffress

This is where the adventure begins! Having done the work outlined above, we're now ready to set course for the next chapter of our lives. In order to develop a new design, I recommend each person follow three steps:

1. The first--and truly most important--step is to establish your priorities.
    a. Ask yourself, what do you want to keep from your current attachments? As you've looked at your current attachments, there are things that are important to you. Those things need to remain in your plan.
    b. Then, what do you want to add in from the things that maybe you've set aside or been sacrificing?
    c. Finally, what do you want to bring into your life to work towards those lifetime dreams?

These questions will take time to evaluate and define, but they are the essential foundation for moving towards a new start.

2. Step two is to ask yourself, what are your minimum needs and are they being met?
    a. What must you do to ensure that you can maintain a healthy and satisfactory lifestyle?

As you are building your plan, make sure ensure that you are taking care of the basics.

3. Step three is to ask yourself what resources you have available
    to launch your plan.
    a. Resources include: finances; friends; family;
        employment; facilities; contacts, etc.

Wright

Well this is some introspective stuff isn't it? Not for the lighthearted.

Jeffress

David, although this requires a great deal of effort, the introspection
will pay off significantly. There are tremendous benefits from determining
what is of greatest value to us – and, then in the pursuit of that new
awareness.

Wright

Once someone answers these questions how do they get started
moving forward?

Jeffress

David, moving forward requires our readers to ask themselves each and
every day, "What is one action step that I can take today?" Many of our
readers will be familiar with the teaching of Lao-Tzu that says, "A journey
of a thousand miles begins with a single step." It is not possible to do
everything all at one time. That is the purpose of completing step one,
"What are your priorities?" The value of the other steps is to determine
what is feasible now. The daily activity of examining at least one thing you
can do is to get you putting one foot in front of the other and taking
action. No matter how difficult things may seem initially, believe it or not
you are in control. You control yourself; you control what you think, what
you care about, what you do, and who you surround yourself with.

Wright

Lyn you've titled this particular chapter in our book, "Yes You Can Start
Over." Does every change require a restart?

Jeffress

No. I don't think that every change requires somebody to start over. However, what I do believe is that every change is an opportunity to do the kind of personal examination that helps you determine what you want to put into the next chapter of your life.

I recommend making a practice of looking at the three questions I've outlined earlier in this chapter: "What are my attachments" "What am I sacrificing?" "What are my dreams?" Doing this on a regular basis provides the ability to be agile and excited as each challenge comes along.

Wright

You know every time I go into some sort of a planning session, either personally or for my business, I enter it with a real positive attitude, which makes it a little difficult to admit there might be some detours, some setbacks, but I imagine that there would be setbacks in what you're talking about. So how does one deal with them?

Jeffress

David I know this may sound overly optimistic, but I believe setbacks are inevitable. In my opinion, setbacks are all part of life's adventure. I will suggest to our readers that it is helpful to treat setbacks as a way to learn new ways of living your lives.

I have several recommendations for our readers. My goal would be for each person to become the orchestrator of his/her own destiny...for each person to enjoy life--even with all its challenges and opportunities.

- My first recommendation: Ground your plan; make it visible. Don't just leave your plan to float around inside your head. I suggest that you use photos that inspire you, listen to music that moves you, create a collage or draw a picture. The objective is to get your plan out there as a living entity for you to see.

- My second recommendation: Revisit your priorities on a regular basis. Following the guidelines that I have outlined for dealing with change or loss, you will find that your priorities will change and you will want to adjust to those changes. Be sure to set a daily focus of action. Remember, a setback just requires a new action step.

- Another recommendation is to give yourself a break! We only get one chance at life and we need to enjoy it! Things will not always go perfectly. Try to bring as much fun and laugher into your life as you can. Get together with friends, go see comedies, read just for pleasure, and get out into nature.
- The last recommendation I'm going to make may be the most important one. Pay attention to *what is working* and know that *you* brought that success about.

Wright

I was going to ask you if you had any last words, but that almost sounds like you've done that.

Jeffress

I cannot say this enough—the focus needs to be on taking action. I recently reread one of Peter Block's books, *The Answer to How is Yes.* I was reminded of the power of action versus inaction. Block out questions like, "How will I—?" When we ask that kind of a question, we are telling ourselves that we don't have access to the answer. We're saying we are stuck. We are telling ourselves that the answers lie outside of our own experience. As long as we remain inactive, we feel as though we are not in the driver's seat. Therefore, my closing advice is:

Do something each day!

Movement toward your goals will continue to reveal what is important and possible in your life. Know this: You are in control of your own life. Do not give up that control to others.

Wright

What you said really hit me—things are outside of your experience. What would be wrong with getting mentors—people who have had the experience I haven't had? Is that a possibility?

Jeffress

Oh absolutely. David, even the act of finding a mentor or finding somebody who has had an experience that you haven't is an action step. What I'm cautioning against is putting yourself in that state of "action paralysis." It's the act of standing still, of allowing yourself to be inactive during a time of change or loss that leads a person to feel badly. On the other hand, taking action begins to change that experience and frees you up to moving forward.

Wright

Well what a great conversation I really appreciate all the time that you've spent with me in answering these questions, you've given me a lot to think about, and I'm sure that our readers are going to not only be moved into action by this chapter, but introspection is always great and I do appreciate you bringing it to the forefront for us.

Jeffress

Thank you. I am hopeful that our discussion will help our readers see that, "Yes, You Can" start over and enjoy what life is presenting to you. I appreciate the time that we have spent talking about the steps our readers can follow to take charge of their own lives.

Wright

Today we've been talking to Lyn Jeffress; she is the Founder and President of Imagined Future Inc., a coaching, consulting, and training company. Through her work there at Imagined Future she has helped teams, individuals, teams, and organizations discover and maximize their performance. Lyn thank you so much for being with us today on Yes You Can.

Jeffress

Thank you David.

Lyn Jeffress is Founder and President of Imagined Future, Inc.™, a coaching, consulting, and training organization. Lyn's passion is helping others discover and release their potential and live the life they've only dreamed of.

Lyn holds both a master's degree in Leadership and an MBA. In addition, Lyn received her coaching certification from the Hudson Institute and has had the honor of studying with visionary thinkers such as Martin Seligman, Stephen R. Covey, David L. Cooperrider, as well as movie producer, Stephen Simon.

Through the work of Imagined Future, Inc. Lyn helps individuals, teams, and organizations discover and maximize their performance. Her work with teams results in increased understanding of the potential of each member. She also helps to shift paradigms within organizations in order to improve the contribution of each team to the organization.

Lyn Jeffress
12932 SE Kent-Kangley Road, Suite 255
Kent, WA 98030
253-239-1387
lynj@imaginedfuture.com
www.imaginedfuture.com

CHAPTER 14

Reaching Beyond Your Greatest Potential Through the *Power* of *You!*

by Dr. Monica Hardy

"Everything you need to succeed is already on the inside of you; all you need is for someone to activate or stir up the gift."

Wright (Wright)

Today we're talking with Dr. Monica Hardy. Dr. Hardy is a multi-talented professional with expertise in health care, adult education, and human resource development. She is the Senior Pastor of Love, Peace, and Joy Temple of Jesus Christ, the Founder and CEO of Résumés and Beyond Inc., and an area chair and lead instructor at the University of Phoenix. Dr. Hardy has earned a bachelor's degree, dual master's degrees, and dual doctorate degrees. She is a Registered Health Information Administrator and a member of Delta Sigma Theta Sorority Incorporated. Dr. Hardy is also a member of various professional associations and the recipient of several noteworthy honors and awards.

Dr. Hardy, welcome to *Yes You Can!*

Monica Hardy (Hardy)

Thank you; I am honored to be here.

Wright

So how do you see *you* in the mirror?

Hardy

I see myself as outgoing, energetic, motivated, and successful. I'm so glad you asked me this question. Many times people do not know what they are or who they are—they allow others to define them.

One Sunday, I preached a sermon titled "God, I Am What You See." The purpose of the message was to teach the importance of faith and having a vision. If I had to give an illustrative example, it would be an elephant looking in the mirror and the reflection being that of a donkey.

Many times, when I interview my clients prior to preparing their résumé, I ask, "How do you see you?" Others may see you in a certain way, but it doesn't matter how other people see you. It's important to know how you see yourself. Sight is important because sight is vision, and without vision, people perish. Therefore, if you have vision, you have sight, and if you know who you are when you look in the mirror, you're halfway there.

Wright

One of my favorite advertisements is a picture of a tiny kitty cat looking in a mirror and the image in the mirror is a lion.

Hardy

Exactly. That's the whole point of asking the question how you see yourself in the mirror. If you're that elephant, then you feel pretty big, but if you see yourself as a donkey, then that could mean you see yourself smaller or shy. Another thought is you may feel small, but when you look in the mirror you see the lion instead if the kitty. So you are actually bigger than you think.

I like to stress to my clients, my students, and to the members of my congregation, instead of putting so much emphasis on what others see, what *you* see is more important.

Wright

Some would say that we are "fearfully and wonderfully made," so what makes people unique?

Hardy

I have come to realize that if you don't know what you value then you don't really know what you want to do or become in life. This basically means you cannot answer what I call the five W's in life—the who, the what, the when, the where, and the why.

When I say people are fearfully and wonderfully made, there are things about each of us that make us unique. Most of them stem from a set of values that were rooted in us from childhood.

There are many different types of values—there are terminal values and instrumental values. Terminal values are those that question whether you want a comfortable life, how you feel about equality, freedom, harmony, self-esteem, or social recognition. Instrumental values are ambition, being broad-minded, courageous, honest, polite, or having self-control.

So as you can see, the average person has at least two sets of values. If people have not taken the time to self-assess and analyze their values, when they try to move forward in life or try to get that "big time" career, they won't know where to start. Many people are so focused on money that they end up applying for a position that goes totally against everything they believe. It's very important to me for people to take inventory of what's locked on the inside of them. Therefore, when I say you're fearfully and wonderfully made, I'm actually asking what makes you tick?

I believe there is something different about each and every one of us that we should be very honored about. If you are an introvert, why would you apply for a position that keeps you on the front line? Just because that person likes a quieter, inclusive setting does not mean he or she is not needed. Unfortunately, if you haven't taken the time to self-assess and really look at your values, how will you know your unique attributes?

Wright

What do you want to be when you "grow up"?

Hardy

This is the question that generates so many laughs when I ask that of my résumé clients during the interview consultation. When they laugh, I respond with, "You laugh at that question, but when you were six years old you answered it without hesitation. Now that you are an adult, you have no idea of what you want to be when you grow up."

The reason I ask this question is to help people become familiar with their TASK—Talents, Abilities, Skills, and Knowledge. When I ask what they want to be when they grow up, I'm asking, "Do you know what your talents are? Do you know your abilities, your true skill sets? How much wealth/knowledge have you obtained?" This is slightly different from values, now I'm tapping into the things that they have learned—things many people are not giving themselves credit for on a résumé.

One example that comes to mind is when clients come to me for résumé service but prior to the appointment they will erase some parts of their résumé. They will say, "I removed that job or that school because I was not there long or I did not finish, so it's not important."

I happen to think there are relevance, value, and skills in the smallest things. Whether a person graduated from a college or not, all education is important. For example, a client comes in with an ultimate goal to be a chef. However, the client deleted the part of his or her work history were the client served as a shift manager at several major fast food restaurants (McDonalds, Burger King or Wendy's). The first thing that would catch my attention is the fact that this client just threw away years of experience in food management when the goal is to become a chef. I would advise the client not to delete or take anything off his or her resume without professional career advisement. I've had to stress to my clients in situations like this that they need to know their *TASK*. The tasks acquired at McDonalds were more than flipping burgers and saying "may I help you please?" While working in fast food, you can acquire skills and knowledge in food preparation, sterilization, finance, and customer relations.

Wright

So how do you work with people when you ask them, "What would you do if you *could* not fail?"

Hardy

This is a risk factor question. There are two types of careers in everyone. The first type of career is the position we have pursued to obtain a nice paycheck. This is where most of us work for someone else. We go to this job every day and, to be honest, we do it because it pays the bills. Then there is the job you probably do at home that no one knows you do. It's what you *really* love to do, but you won't do it full-time because you're thinking you may not be successful.

I was reading a book once about a CEO who was well known as a CEO, but what people did not know was that he loved to go home and cook. So, that raised the question—if he thought he could not fail, why wouldn't he become a chef?

There are so many people who have things they love to do but are afraid to pursue them. Just before this interview, you and I had a conversation about your music. I could hear in your voice that you really love music. I always say everybody has that second or third avocation that they really love, and sometimes there is a risk factor keeping them from pursuing that activity full-time.

One of my biggest dreams was to open my own business. For years, I worked in management in the healthcare industry and did very well, but my heart was always passionate about helping people. For so long, I feared opening my business as a standalone entity, so I functioned as a consultant. However, today I am so blessed to have been afforded the opportunity to get a building for my business. I have always been a little afraid. I wondered, "What if I do this and fail? What if I get in this building and cannot pay the rent?" or "What if people do not come?" Despite my fears, I realized that sometimes you have to go for it!

Wright

So what about the question, "What would you do if you could not get paid?"

Hardy

This is a question that speaks to passion. It is very similar to the question, "What would you do if you could not fail?" However, I think this is a greater question because even when you are doing something you love, you still need to get paid. This question makes you think about where your heart is. It makes people question whether they really love their job. At the end of the day, one must ask, "How do you feel?" and "Did I make a difference?"

Prior to sitting down to prepare a résumé for clients, I talk to them about their lives and careers. Despite the number of hours I spend with them, some cannot afford my services; but I provide the service anyway because I love what I do. I love speaking into people's lives and helping people to change their lives. It is my heart's desire for people to know that there is something special on the inside of them, and I want to be the person to help them reach their greatest potential.

My business slogan is "Reaching beyond your greatest potential through the power of you." I tell people every day, "I can make you sound very good on paper, but it is *not* what I write that makes the difference. What makes the difference is *you*—how well you present yourself, how well you interview, or how well you think of yourself."

In all the years I worked in healthcare, the one thing that bothered me was at the end of the day I felt I was not making a difference. I would look at my calendar and see where I checked off a meeting here or a meeting there, but I had to ask myself what did I really accomplish at the end of the day? Now things are different—at the end of the day, I've encouraged someone or have lifted someone up. So when people ask what would they do if they could not get paid, that's what I want them to think about—what's really in their hearts.

Wright

So how can people unlearn learned behavior?

Hardy

There are times when we don't know when to step out of the box. When you think of all the questions previously asked, society has us pigeonholed to think one way. What would you do if you could not fail, and what would you do if you could not get paid are two questions that force you to think out of the box. Society has created a set of rules, but do we know when to step away from those rules? Do we know when to be ourselves? Do we know when to say, "Okay, that's enough; I'm going to try something new?" It is important that we unlearn learned behaviors. Now, some rules are in place for a reason; however, sometimes we have to step out of the box—we must unlearn those very rigid ways of thinking.

I asked my students one night in a human resources class, "Would you hire the well-dressed idiot or the purple-headed genius?" Everyone paused, and then some students immediately said, "I would have to hire the well-dressed idiot." When I asked why, they responded, "Because society says that when you walk in the door you are to have on a suit and a tie." Here is where I challenged my students to think outside the box. I said to them, "Think about it: Here you have a candidate who has purple hair and a tattoo, but he is the most qualified candidate. If you step outside the box and go with the unlearned learned behavior theory, you can hire the smarter person and possibly implement a dress code policy to minimize the visibility of odd appearances. So many times we have done the opposite because society says so or because inside this box is a certain set of standards that allows us to remain in our comfort zone."

Wright

You ask your clients to tell you their "commercial." Tell me about that.

Hardy

I ask my clients, "Do you have 'elevator talk'?" The greater portion of life is not what you know; it's who you know. Some of our greatest opportunities are in the weirdest places. When I say to my clients, "Let me hear your commercial," what I want to know is, "When you are on an elevator and you see someone dressed very nicely, has it ever occurred to you that you may be standing next to a CEO? What happens when you walk to your car and you see the owner of the company drop his or her keys in the parking lot? If you rush over to assist, do you have a sixty-second commercial ready?"

A sixty-second commercial gives the prospective employer a glimpse of who you are. Even if you are nervous, it would sound something like this, "Hi, how are you today? My name is Dr. Monica Hardy, and I noticed that you work upstairs on the sixth floor in the marketing department. I just wanted you to know that I have a background in marketing, and here are my areas of expertise and some of my accomplishments." During a sixty-second commercial, people have the ability to, on demand, say their name and a little bit about their education, profession, and area of expertise, as well as any results-based accomplishments right there on the spot. Sixty-second commercials are not easy. They require practice, but they also leave a greater impression.

Wright

These are great questions that you ask your clients, so let's continue. Another question you ask is, "Everyone around you is a bird, but are you an eagle or a chicken?" Tell me about this question.

Hardy

I receive a large volume of e-mails daily. I was reading a particular e-mail and I thought it was one of *the* most profound things I have read. The e-mail read something like this: "You have two birds, and these two birds are friends. These birds decided to walk together to the very end, and they decided that they would never turn around—no matter what. On the path, these two birds were having fun. They felt good, and they laughed. Still, each of these birds had different feathers. Somehow they still managed to walk together. When they were walking together, they did not realize they had different minds; they were birds but they were different kinds of birds.

"Then they came to a place on their path where they had to make a decision because the path had come to an end. They had to determine whether they would stay or fly high to get to the other side. One bird said to the other bird, 'Come on, we're together on this; let's go to the other side!' But the other bird said, 'No, I'm not going. I'm not leaving this ground! I'm not going to take off and soar in the air; are you crazy?' Then it dawned on the other bird that he was an eagle and the other bird was a chicken."

Now, that was a short version of the story, but when I read it I thought, "Wow, there are some people in this life who are just not meant to go everywhere with you." So many of my clients are disappointed when their relationships began to change. They want to take everybody with them. When they lose friends or they get promotions and start advancing in life, some people they thought were friends are no longer with them. Remember, everyone you count you can't count on.

I find it easy to counsel people in this situation because I know the feeling well. I do not hesitate to tell them, "It's not because these people don't like you or they don't desire to go, they just can't because you're an eagle and they are chickens."

It is my desire to encourage my clients and even those reading this book that "Yes you can" have all the success you deserve and desire. Great success sometimes comes at a cost. You may at times find yourself walking alone, but don't be dismayed—eagles fly alone.

Wright

That's a great story.

Another question you ask your clients is, "Most people prefer a pen, but why should you prefer a pencil?"

Hardy

This is another awesome story that I actually heard in church. One night while at church, the guest speaker started his message by sharing a Norwegian proverb. It was about a pencil maker talking to some pencils as he packed them up to be sent away. As the speaker began to share, I began to write because I consider these golden nuggets that can be used in various aspects of life. Of course, I incorporated a few of these nuggets in my business to help my clients understand that no matter what, "yes you can" make it. Because the business world prefers a pen, I challenge my client to think outside the box and unlearn learned behavior. I ask the client to ask why he or she should think like a pencil. The answers could be:

1. You will only be effective if you are in powerful hands, so we need to make sure that we connect ourselves to powerful people. Always try to be around someone who is more powerful or more successful than you.

2. When you get dull you may experience a painful sharpening but it won't kill you. It will only make you stay on point. In other words, there are going to be things in your life that are going to be very painful and most of the time they happen to you when you get "dull" or down. This means you get comfortable, you get bored, or things tend to become one way in your life. Then all of a sudden, a "kairos moment" will happen. It will make you stand up on your feet and take notice. A kairos moment is an unexpected event (sometimes painful) that will drastically change things in your life (i.e., death or birth) to get you back on course.

3. As a pencil, you have the ability to correct your own mistakes. Just turn yourself upside down and whatever mistakes you made, you can erase them. Many times when we make a mistake we think it's over, but if you think like a pencil you can just simply erase or just simply start over to have a fresh start.

4. The most important part of you is on the inside. It doesn't matter what you look like on the outside—the "lead of the pencil" is on the inside and that's purpose! Once again, this makes me think about my business slogan and what I want my clients to keep in mind—you can reach beyond your greatest potential through the power of you. Everything you need is on the inside of you!

5. Wherever you go, leave your mark! Wherever you've been, people will know that you have been there. A pencil can leave a different mark than a pen; it does not have any color, but sometimes a simple touch is all that's needed. You only get one time to leave a first impression so make it good!

6. The last thing so awesome about a pencil is that even if you break, you can still write because you have ability even in your brokenness. If a pen breaks, you can't use it anymore, but if you break a pencil in half, you can sharpen it and use it.

Wright

Money can buy a lot of things, but not everything; so what motivates you?

Hardy

I have come to realize that the number one reason we seek employment is for the salary. However, as we grow and mature, we find out that money is not everything. At some point in life, you start wanting peace of mind, self-actualization, growth, and maturity; it's not always about the almighty dollar. When I consult with my clients, I let them know that it is my desire to aid them in establishing a career—not just to find a job. In doing that, they must consider more than the salary.

To support this, I read to my clients a Chinese proverb. I found it to be poignant. I like to have words of wisdom to encourage my clients. Job loss or not being able to find a job can be detrimental to a person's esteem. I also like to encourage my clients to think about more than salary so they can see the value they have inside them. When you do not know your value or your worth, you will stay on a job (though miserable) for a certain dollar amount when you could be worth so much more.

The Chinese proverb is: "You can buy a house, but not a home. You can buy a clock, but you can't buy time. You can buy a bed, but you can't buy sleep. You can buy a book, but you can't buy knowledge. You can pay for a doctor, but you can't buy good health. You can pay for a position, but you can't buy respect. You can buy blood, but you can't buy life. Finally, you can pay for sex, but you cannot buy love." We place so many emphases on money, but without priority, we must ask ourselves what's the real value?

Wright

Tell us about the next question you ask your clients: who do people say you are?

Hardy

I definitely could not end this interview without this question. This question speaks to character. To me, you're not anything if you do not have good character. Actually, "Who Do People Say That You Are" was a sermon title from a message that I preached at church. I always say to people, "You say you are a Christian, but who do other people say you are?" That is so important because we see ourselves a certain way, which is good, but we also want someone to agree with us, especially when it comes to our character, integrity, being a good, upright person, and keeping our commitments.

All you have is your word, so when you say you're going to do something, do it! One thing is for sure—once you say you're a Christian or you're a good person, people want to see what kind of fruit you are producing on your tree.

Many of my clients have told me that when they sit down with me it is like a mild interrogation because I am challenging them to analyze themselves. If they say they are a leader I want to know, are they really leading or are they following? I want them to be able to articulate leadership qualities. The Bible says, "Let your yea be yea and your nay be nay..." (Matthew 5:37 and James 5:12). With that being said, I want others to see who my clients say they are.

Wright

Well, what a great conversation. I've really enjoyed this conversation today with you. I think this is going to be a very good addition to our book, and I appreciate all this time you've taken to answer these questions.

Hardy

I thank you so much, David, for the opportunity.

Wright

This morning we have been talking with Dr. Monica Hardy. Dr. Hardy is a mother of two, a Senior Pastor, a health information administrator, educator, and business owner. As Founder and CEO of Résumés & Beyond Inc., she specializes in professional development, résumé writing, career and academic advertisement, training, and motivational speaking. Dr. Hardy is a sought-after speaker in the community, academically, professionally, and spiritually. Her focus is redirecting and touching lives by helping people realize that their greatest potential is locked on the inside them.

Dr. Hardy, thank you so much for being with us today on *Yes You Can!*

Hardy

Thank you.

ABOUT THE AUTHOR

Dr. Monica Hardy is a mother of two, a senior pastor, a Registered Health Information Administrator, an educator, and a business owner. As the Founder and CEO of Résumés & Beyond, Inc., she specializes in professional development, résumé writing, career and academic advisement, training, and motivational speaking. Dr. Hardy is a sought-after speaker in the community, academically, professionally and spiritually. Her focus is redirecting and touching lives by helping people realize that their greatest potential is inside them.

Dr. Monica Hardy

Résumés & Beyond, Inc.
10646 Haverford Road, Suite #7
Jacksonville, FL 32218
904-757-5775 Phone
904-757-3770 Fax
resumesandbeyond@bellsouth.net
www.resumesandbeyondinc.com
www.drmhardy.org

CHAPTER 15

Winners are not Simply Motivated—They are Inspired!

by Mike Sarro

David Wright (Wright)

Today we're talking with Mike Sarro. Mike has been a youth sports coach in multiple sports for more than twenty-five years. He strongly believes that coaches have the power to exert a positive influence in the lives of kids through the platform of sports. His coaching style revolves around the compelling Positive Expectations Methodology, which he has developed through years of on-the-job experience. Another key ingredient to Mike's system is seizing the subtle teaching moments that occur every day.

Over the course of his coaching career, Mike has led various teams through local, state, regional, and national levels of competition. He also holds positions of leadership within a variety of sports organizations, leagues, and governing bodies. He is a charter member of the Positive Coach's Alliance, a certified instructor at the state level for several youth sports governing bodies, and belongs to the National Fast Pitch Coach's Association. He is also an active member of the National Speakers Association.

In addition to coaching, Mike is a frequent speaker at coaching clinics, banquets, and seminars. His materials are tailored to address the needs of youth sports coaches.

Mike welcome to *Yes You Can!*

Mike Sarro (Sarro)

Thanks David, it's great to be part of this exciting project.

Wright

So I know you've been coaching youth sports for more than twenty-five years, and you've also evolved into a role of teaching about coaching youth sports. How did you first get into coaching?

Sarro

Just like many other parents, I first became involved as our three kids began to play sports. Initially, I assisted the T-ball team on which my eldest daughter Stephanie played. I remember being impressed by the genuine enthusiasm the kids showed. They learned like little "sponges," taking in everything for the first time. It was amazing how much each player improved in a relatively short time.

The "coaching bug" bit me during that experience, and the rest is history. I continued coaching teams for our younger daughter, Andrea, and our son, Michael. Fortunately (or unfortunately), my kids were on the teams when I was just "cutting my teeth" as a coach." However, I wouldn't change a thing. Those were some of the most fun and gratifying years of my life, with great memories.

Eventually our kids grew up and moved on. However, I've continued to coach girls' fastpitch softball. There is an enormous "natural high" associated with helping young players develop and knowing you've had a positive influence in their lives. That's a feeling that never gets old. My coaching career has now come full circle, as I'm coaching my granddaughter, Gabrielle.

Wright

So let's jump in immediately with a tough question. The term "winner" has got to be among the most misused and wrongly applied terms in sports. From the perspective of a youth sports coach, how should we define a winner?

Sarro

David, that's definitely a hot button for me. Far too many people "crown" winners based on criteria that is misguided, and outside of a young athlete's control. The two most common mistakes are: 1) Putting too much stock on wins and losses; and 2) Unfairly comparing them against other athletes of similar age who are probably at different stages in development.

It's our responsibility to provide every single player—not just the stars—with the guidance and confidence to become better. Kids learn at different speeds and in different modes. Some are blessed with natural athleticism and therefore tend to show their skills early. Throughout the years, I have observed that there is no guarantee these quick-starters will continue to progress at the same pace as their peers. Many kids are late bloomers who eventually surpass a lot of those quick-starters over time. Personally, I can empathize with the late bloomers, because I was one of them. Given this background, let's use three key factors to judge winners;

1. **Effort**—Winners are players who consistently give their best effort, regardless of the circumstances. They are not always the most talented players. However, they show up regularly, work hard, and usually do more than you ask of them. In a team sport, individuals rarely have direct control of their team's wins and losses. However, everyone chooses how hard he or she will work, and how hard he or she will try.

2. **Development**—Winners show steady, measurable improvement in mastering the fundamental skills. Again, they aren't always the most physically gifted players. They improve over time because of their love for the sport, along with the blood, sweat, and tears they are willing to pour into it.

   I've seen many real life examples of so-called "underdogs" emerging into real stars! One in particular was a young teenager named Kate. As a rookie on our fastpitch softball team, she was shy, quiet, and wore thick glasses. As we know, looks can be deceiving. Her relentless work ethic quickly became obvious to everyone, and she would play any role that was asked. One night, our starting (and only) catcher did not show up for a game. We were in a real pinch. At that level of competition, the catcher position is pivotal to team success and very physically demanding. Kate quietly raised her hand, and said she would give it a try. That night, she did amazingly well and became our permanent catcher from that point forward. The rest is history! We won a championship with her anchoring our defense behind home plate. Fast-forwarding even further ahead, Kate became an All-Conference college catcher at the Division II level! It's a classic illustration of how you just never know what power lies within the players right in front of you!

3. **Attitude**—Winners enjoy competing and will always try their best to win. But regardless of the outcome, they show respect and empathy toward their coaches, teammates, opponents, and the officials. Anybody can be a "good sport" when things are going well. Winners are good teammates in all situations.

One final thought: confidence can be extremely fragile with young players. Coaches should continuously look for new ways to build them up. Remind them of the things they're doing well. Feedback is the "breakfast of champions"!

Wright

So what are the critical traits or attributes required to be a successful youth sports coach?

Sarro

First and foremost, you should love the sport that you coach. When you, as the leader, show an obvious passion for the game, it becomes contagious. Your enthusiasm will flow naturally to your players, and it becomes instant motivation.

Take a positive outlook on things, with a "glass is half full" mentality. It's important to keep the big picture in mind when making decisions. Almost anybody can evaluate a player's current skill sets. The great coaches envision players as they *can* be, several years into the future. Many players don't realize or believe in their own potential. Tell them honestly what they can achieve. It may even be in something outside of the sport you're coaching.

Another secret to success is keeping your emotions in check. You just can't allow your mood to rise and fall based the latest game. In my view, this is the single most difficult characteristic to master as a coach! We all have a competitive side and an ego. We all want our teams to win. However, putting the primary focus on winning is extremely counterproductive and leads to frustration. In youth sports, it is most important to focus on the fundamental building blocks that make the players and the team as a whole better. As the collective skill level of the team improves, the wins will come as a result. It's not the other way around.

Another important factor is patience. As mentioned earlier, kids learn at their own pace and in different ways. The coach cannot become easily frustrated when things don't go according to "our" plans. The players will sense this and assume they've let you down in some way. Find out how to ignite that light bulb in each player. There is no cookie-cutter approach here. Very often, extra effort and creativity are required to reach certain players. However, the payoff is very much worth it.

You can *not* be an effective leader and communicator if you're not organized. You need to document and track important things like the team roster, contact info, schedules, practice plans, medical records, equipment inventories, etc.

And finally, it helps to have a little salesmanship in you. Coaches are constantly "selling" the team's core beliefs, practice methodologies, and why we do things a certain way. When coaching older, more competitive players, you'll need to be convincing on lineup structure, playing positions, etc. You are selling them on how the individual puzzle pieces (players) must fit together to build a strong team. And of course, recruiting is also selling.

Wright

So what do you think are the key elements to building a successful team or program?

Sarro

I follow a three-step approach:

Envision the Finished Product—To be an effective leader, the coach needs to have a vision of how the team could or should look by the end of the season.

Once this vision is established, translate that into some clear, measurable goals for everyone to work toward. Before we go any further, let me make one thing very clear: these goals are not in the form of wins and losses. They are actually benchmarks against the fundamental skills, knowledge base, and characteristics that lead to success in your sport.

For example, the vision can be as simple as creating a checklist of five core skills that every player can execute. If everyone on the team performs these skills successfully, the team will improve from top to bottom. To use a basketball example, you could set a target for overall team foul shooting percentage. The logic is that good foul shooting makes the team much better. Since you're measuring it, you will naturally invest practice time on making foul shots.

Another perspective could be setting what I call "growth goals." This could be setting a target for the number of new pitchers who will be groomed to pitch in games this season. Taking on a goal of this type might actually sacrifice some early-season team performance. However, this up-front teaching investment will pay you back in spades later. Good pitchers are a cherished commodity in fastpitch softball and baseball. Good pitching always translates into a decided advantage for your team.

To summarize, envisioning your team as a finished product forces you to think strategically about the upcoming season. This empowers leading your team to that next plateau, since you now know what it looks like. Your expectations should be challenging, yet realistic based the actual makeup of your team.

Document a Master Plan for the Season—Once you can envision the team as a finished product, the next logical step is creating a plan to get there. A Master Plan lists periodic milestones for your team in order to reach the end-of-season vision. A typical youth sports season spans a three to four-month period. Therefore, a Master Plan with monthly milestones could break the season into quarterly segments.

Be sure to include the fun stuff as well. These would be events such as pasta/pizza party, field trips to games, team contests, etc. The fun activities are a key part of the overall team experience, and therefore must be planned. Once completed, this Master Plan becomes your blueprint for the team's practice strategies.

Practice Strategies Follow the Master Plan—The team's practice strategies now revolve around achieving the Master Plan. Every practice has a purpose. Practices are geared toward teaching the skills needed to reach the next milestones. To keep you organized and on schedule, there should be a written practice plan with time targets for each practice. This also helps you better budget the time needed in for each fundamental area.

Let's follow up on some of my previous examples. Setting a target for team foul shooting will obviously cause you to allot practice to work on foul shots. Setting a goal for developing a specific number of new pitchers in softball/baseball will cause you to dedicate significant time and emotional energy in this area. However, these skill sets are critical to success in their respective sports. You ultimately become what you've practiced.

Wright

So what are the most effective ways for a coach to communicate the team's vision and goals to the players, to the coaching staff, and, of course, to the parents?

Sarro

David, you just made an excellent point in mentioning the parents as part of the communications loop, especially in the younger age groups; they play a huge role in the overall equation. As a rule, it's best to start the communication process as soon as possible. A good way to accomplish this is to conduct a mandatory preseason meeting with the players and parents. This is your platform to explain the "rules of engagement" in a positive yet firm manner. The tone should be very positive. Topics to cover will vary, depending on the age of the players and the competition level of the sport. Typically, you would include introductions, your coaching philosophy, and how to properly handle issues that may arise. I view this meeting as a pre-emptive strike against potential misunderstandings and false expectation.

A natural complement to the preseason meeting is a Team Handbook. The handbook is an efficient tool for distributing all of that season startup information. Typically, the handbook can include the team's Mission, the Coach's Welcome Message, Roster, Contact Information, Game Schedule, Letter to the Parents, etc. You may have to invest in some copying costs, but it's well worth it.

A team Web site is also an extremely powerful communication tool. As we all know, even the best plans and schedules can change frequently. A team Web site will save you countless phone calls and e-mails. Anyone with a computer can access the most up-to-date team news, practice and game schedules, 24–7.

In addition, I love to utilize the Web site to deliver inspirational or motivational messages to the team. These are positive thoughts that you want to plant in the minds of your players. Of course, this part is contingent on the age level you are coaching. Many times these messages are written with the parents in mind because they're reading it, too. One final thought: the Web site should never be your primary method for communication. However, it's a great tool to complement or re-enforce what you're already telling the team.

Wright

Practice is obviously a critical element in any sport. With the combination of hectic family schedules and a lack of enough facilities, conducting an effective practice has to be a real challenge. How do you maximize benefits gained from each practice, and what are the biggest obstacles?

Sarro

In the youth sports world, it's a huge challenge to get everyone together for enough time to properly cover all of the fundamentals thoroughly. Our biggest obstacles are a shortage of available field/facility time, conflicting school activities, the weather, and sometimes injuries. Teams that get the most "bang" out of their practice time will have a decided competitive advantage.

With that as background, the critical elements for an effective practice are:

The Coach Sets the Standard. Nobody should outwork you. Always start with a written practice plan. You can't just roll out the equipment and hope for the best. Every activity should have a purpose. A written plan forces you to think out how you can get the maximum benefit for all players within the allotted time.

Practices Mirror your Season Master Plan. As we covered earlier, the team's practice strategies are tied into the monthly milestones that were set. The goals can always be tweaked as the season progresses. The practices should then remain in sync with the overall plan.

Maximize the Time. Separate the team into small groups for a portion of the practice. The groups should rotate simultaneously through "stations" that are geared for specific skill sets. Typically, the time spent at each station can range from seven to fifteen minutes. This approach enables you to maximize the number of repetitions executed by each player. It also minimizes waiting or down time significantly. Stations are manned by coaches or qualified helpers. Obviously, having more qualified helpers enables you run more simultaneous stations.

For a practical example, let's use hitting in softball or baseball. Separate stations could be set up to focus on individual elements such as bat grip, wrist turns, hip turns and footwork. Stations could also be set up for live pitching, bunting, strike zone recognition, etc. When it's time for everyone to rotate to the next station, the coach can blow a whistle, sound an air horn, or just yell out a verbal cue. The bottom line: maximize the time your players are actually executing something and eliminate all unnecessary waiting or down time.

Incorporate the "Speed of the Game"—How many times have we heard a coach bemoan his or her team's inability to execute something during games, yet claim to practice it frequently? It's probably because these coaches don't execute the drills at real-time speed in which things occur during the games. It's important to incorporate game-like speeds and stress levels into all practices. Adding elements such as competing against the clock, intra-squad competitions, or hitting live pitching will give players the best chance possible to be "game ready."

Simulate Key Game Situations—As a follow-up to the previous point, it's also important to practice the scenarios most likely to occur during games. A big mistake made by many coaches is assuming the players will know what to do if the situation occurs. This is simply not realistic! If you don't practice something, it's not fair to just expect them to execute it in competition.

I have a funny example to emphasize this point. Several years back, we competed regularly against a league arch rival that had a loud and boisterous head coach on the sidelines. This particular season we had talented players, but a young and unseasoned team. Each time we played that team, our players seemed to get intimidated and distracted. It was mostly due that coach's noise and theatrics. We lost all of the regular season games to that team. Sure enough, come playoff time we are heading for another showdown against our nemesis. We decided to take a radical approach at practice the day prior to that game. The entire practice was executed with a volunteer parent yelling and moving around on the sidelines, imitating that coach. It was hilarious and had everyone in stitches. We played that team the next evening and, of course, the coach started his usual antics. Only this time, our players were smiling and giggling. It now seemed funny, since he was acting just like we had practiced it. Needless to say, we won that game!

Keep it Interesting—Obviously it's important to spend plenty of time mastering the core skills of your sport. But constantly repeating the same drills will become boring and tedious for everyone. Find ways to add creative wrinkles into the basic drills. This can be something as simple as using a different ball or multiple colors that should trigger different action. Make it a variation from the mundane.

Feedback is the Breakfast of Champions—I mentioned this earlier. It's important to re-enforce the drills and activities with constructive feedback done in a positive manner. Also, it's important to end each practice by summarizing "here's what we accomplished today" with the team.

Wright

You frequently use the phrase "fundamentals begin with *F-U-N*. What is the trick to balancing the fun aspects with the working hard aspects of learning the core skills?

Sarro

Youth sports are supposed to be fun. During some of the previous questions, we discussed the ways to reap the maximum benefits out of practices. This often requires a lot of hard work, so it's really important to include activities that keep the "Fun Meter" buzzing. There are creative ways to make practices both instructional *and* fun.

For starters, create team contests that incorporate fundamental drills along with friendly competition. For example, we created a "Team Gladiator" contest. This is a direct knock-off of the *American Gladiator* show on television. The players are sent through an obstacle course, which is a continuous series of drill stations. Of course, they are competing against the clock as they navigate their way through the obstacles. The best overall time wins a prize. As you can see, a fun contest can be created out of almost any activity. All you need is a little imagination and the guts to try it.

Other ideas could include a team pasta or pizza party, an excursion to watch a college game in your sport, or fun review quizzes at the end of practice. Believe it or not, the kids love the quizzes. And of course, let's not forget those ice cream or water ice excursions following a hot game or practice.

Wright

One of the most intimidating challenges for youth sports coaches has to be working with and getting along with parents. What are the secrets to success here?

Sarro

To some coaches, dealing with the parents is by far the most intimidating part of the job. This is due to a *small but vocal* percentage of parents who view the youth sports world through tunnel-vision glasses. They see things only through the eyes of their child. Objectivity is not necessarily within their vocabulary. Their child is "obviously" the star of this team. They don't understand why the coaches and other players aren't genuflecting! Unfortunately, we hear far too many horror stories attributed to this very small minority of parents. At minimum, they are high maintenance and require a disproportionate amount of our time. At their worst, they become confrontational with coaches, badger the officials, and don't mix well with the other parents. Thankfully, the vast majority of people don't act this way.

I've been blessed over the years to have worked with lots of terrific parents. In fact, many of them have become some of my best friends. For the most part, parents will support you if their young player is having fun, getting along with the others, and learning something.

However, having an overall positive experience with your team's parents does not happen by accident. There are several proactive steps you must take as the coach and leader of the team. They are:

Avoid Drafting Players with High-Maintenance Parents. Throughout the years, I have avoided drafting some very talented players due to the baggage that comes with their parents. Picking the wrong families can make for a long, miserable season. We don't always know the families in advance. Therefore, obtaining this info requires some homework on your part. Think about this: coaches spend a lot of energy in gathering scouting reports on prospective players for the team. Why not carry it one step further? Create a "scouting report" so to speak, on players' parents.

This information can be obtained by speaking with past coaches of these players or friends who can give you the scoop.

Set Expectations for the Parents. Several years ago, I discovered an excellent article written by Dr. Moe Gelbart, Clinical Psychologist, and Clinical Director of PsychCare Alliance. The main point of the article was to educate parents on the difference between "Involvement" and "Interference." This article has since become a standard attachment to my preseason letter that is sent to every parent. One very interesting tidbit from Dr. Gelbart's article was advising parents to "act like your child's parent, not their agent!"

Wright

As a coach it's obviously important to have good knowledge of the playing rules for your sport. Aside from trying to memorize those painfully dry and tedious rule books, are there any tricks to learning the most critical rules quickly?

Sarro

Yes, there are, actually. One thing I recommend is to attend an umpire's, referee's, or official's workshop. If at all possible, take it one step further and obtain at least the first level of certification. Become a certified umpire, referee, or game official. As you can imagine, understanding the rules becomes more critical as you move up through the older, higher age levels with higher competition. In addition, the game officials seem to recognize and respect the coaches who take the time to understand the rules.

I have a quick, funny little anecdote here. Sometimes good intentions can work against you. Years ago, I took the time to become a certified umpire. Once during an important tournament game, I felt that a rule had been misapplied in a situation. Obviously, the call went against us. When discussing it with the umpire-in-chief, I informed him of my knowledge of that rule because "I'm a certified umpire." He immediately interpreted this to mean that I knew the rules better than he did. Needless to say, that discussion was over quickly and it did not go in my favor. Looking back, it wasn't necessarily *what* I said, but probably *how* I said it!

Wright

So what is the best way to teach players about good sportsmanship and showing respect for the opponents and officials?

Sarro

That is an excellent question. As a coach and leader, it all begins with you. Let me repeat that *it all begins with you!* Good or bad, you will lead by example. If you show respect for the other team and for the game officials, the players will generally follow your lead. On the other hand, if you are constantly chirping at the officials or complaining about close calls, the players will feel entitled to do it as well. This even extends to your keeping assistant coaches and sometimes your fans under control.

There will always be times of adversity during competition. Teach your players how to manage adversity. Teaching this process to players is just as important as the other fundamental skills. Players must learn to stay focused on the factors within their own control. Examples include their attitude, whether they hustle, and how hard they try. On the other hand, there is little point in wasting energy over factors outside of our control. Examples include the weather, the official's calls, or the actions of other people. There will always be times when we perceive the official's calls to be going against us. When coaches lose control of their emotions in these situations, they set a poor example, and take their team's focus away from the game. I've witnessed many examples where a team lost a game that they should have won, simply due to losing focus because of a perceived bad call. Once that elusive focus is lost, it's difficult to get it back. Teams that learn to control their emotions properly during these situations will always have a competitive edge.

Wright

As the coach, you're responsible for the safety and well-being of your team. How do you go about keeping everyone safe?

Yes You Can!

Sarro

In my experience, there are three distinct layers to safety. They are: 1) preventing injuries, 2) reacting to injuries when they happen, and 3) cultivating a safe and non-threatening atmosphere. Here are some quick thoughts on each:

- To help prevent injuries, follow the pre-existing safety rules established by your league or governing body. These rules are usually well documented and it's vital to follow them. You should avoid conducting drills or activities that are too advanced for the age or current skill set of the players on the team. Lastly, ensure that the playing field or facility is well-maintained and free of obvious safety hazards.

- When injuries inevitably happen, it's important to have an action plan in mind. This action can be as simple as calling 911. All coaches should take courses in first aid and CPR. In the event of a serious injury, these courses teach you how to react during the critical minutes until help arrives. These courses are very often provided free of charge by your league or the local municipality.

- As the team leader, you must cultivate a non-threatening, "safe haven" type of atmosphere for your players. This means avoiding inappropriate physical contact, as well as off-color comments or jokes. Never put yourself (or others) in a situation where you are "one-on-one" with young players. General coaching activities should always be conducted in open space, and in plain view. If you must have a behind-doors conversation, be sure at least one other adult is present. Always have your eyes open and be aware of the people around you. And finally, ensure that everyone feels "welcome" and that he or she is an important part of the team.

Wright

So what are some tips for maximizing the team's performance on game day?

Sarro

There is a two-part answer to that question. First, it's important to *get* everyone physically, and mentally ready to play the game. Secondly you must help to *keep* everyone in ready mode through the entire course of the game.

Helping the team *get* ready begins from the moment they arrive at the field. It sounds like a simple concept, but it's not always that easy. Players will often show up for games in various states of mind, and not always in "game ready" mode. Particularly with older age groups, their mood can depend on what happened earlier in school or at home. Therefore, it's important to execute a familiar and repeatable pregame routine. Start with dynamic warm-up exercises that are applicable to your sport. Follow that immediately with light walk-throughs of the core fundamental skills. Some last-minute reviews of specific goals or strategies for this game can also be done. It's important to have these routines coordinated among the coaches so that everyone carries out his or her role when the team arrives.

The second part is *keeping* them game-ready throughout the entire contest. We've discussed some of these techniques in an earlier question. Teach the team to stay focused on the things they can control, and minimize distractions of elements that are outside their control. This includes helping players overcome the mistakes that will inevitably occur during a game.

I've got a silly but effective illustration of how this can be done. As you know, players often get upset after committing an error. If we allow them to dwell on their mistakes, they'll shut down mentally for the rest of the game. To help prevent this, we demonstrate the "flush it" technique. You push the imaginary handle on the side of your head and then imitate the sound of a toilet flushing. You can jazz up the visual effects with a little extra body language. I've used this routine for years. It almost always gets the player to laugh or at least smile a little. Most importantly, you've provided them with a visual picture of their mistake going down the drain. They're now liberated to forget it, and move on. Before long, the players do the routine themselves. As you can imagine, you can really have some fun with it.

Wright

Up to this point we've discussed lots of things that coaches should do. Just as importantly, perhaps, we should discuss the things that coaches must *not* do. You've compiled a list of your "seven deadly sins" of youth sports coaching. Would you tell our readers what they are?

Sarro

Yes, the "Seven Deadly Sins" are my short list of behaviors that lead coaches to failure. As you will see, we've discussed several of these already.

1. *Failure to define your vision, philosophy, and expectations up front.* We discussed this at length earlier. If you don't communicate these "standard operating procedures" *before* the season starts, you will travel down that crooked path of misunderstanding and unmet expectations.

2. *Being a "Daddy" or "Mommy" Coach.* We've all seen it. These are people who coach to ensure their child plays his or her favorite positions, and gets the most playing time. As a parent-coach, treat your child like everyone else, and treat everyone else like your child.

3. *Allowing "I" Infections.* You can *never* allow a few divas or prima donnas to dictate how things will get done. The same rules must apply to everyone. If allowed, these few "chosen ones" will ruin team chemistry and undermine your authority.

4. *Expecting the team to perform something that they have not practiced.* You need to practice a skill/play multiple times, at game speed. In addition, you must ensure all the players understand *why* they are doing it.

5. *Negative Coaching.* This is when a coach thinks he or she can be negative but expect the team to be positive. One of the worst things to ever do is yell at or insult the kids. Coaching can sometimes be a frustrating process that will be challenging, but we need to remember that we are teachers and role models.

6. *Focusing on results only, and not the process.* In youth sports it is mission-critical to place our focus on the fundamental building blocks that make the players and team better. As the collective skill level of the team improves, the wins will come as a result. It's not the other way around.

7. *"Crossing the line" on your Role as Coach.* You are their coach and *not* their parent (with the exception of your own kids). In addition, you cannot be perceived as their best friend. You will constantly encounter kids who don't appear to have a strong support system and are therefore vulnerable. *Never* abuse their trust or put yourself into a compromising position.

Wright

Will you give some examples of what you mean by the expression, "don't just coach—inspire!"?

Sarro

Yes. Coaching at its highest level is when your players are not only motivated, but also inspired. Each individual on your team is good at something. I'm referring more to intangible character traits here, and not necessarily the physical skills. These are traits such as enthusiasm, leadership, reliability, or a cool composure. Find these intangible skills in each of your players and tell him or her about it. Take it one step further by explaining how that trait will help make the child successful later in life. In a way, you are helping your team members define their identity and nurture dreams for the future.

Confidence in kids can be so fragile. They may not believe in their own strengths until they hear it from someone else. Needless to say, you must be sincere and completely honest for this to be effective.

I'll give some examples. On various teams, we've had Christina the "cerebral pitcher," Mallory the motivational speaker, "can do" Halli, "Roadrunner" Allison, Jess the RinkRat, "Fearless" Joanna, and "Underdog" Arlyn. (By the way, "rinkrat" is an ice hockey term, affectionately bestowed on players who never leave the rink.)

Wright

Over the years, you've coached both girls' and boys' youth sports teams. What is the major difference between the two?

Sarro

Great question, David! I can answer that question with two simple but telling sentences. "The boys need to play good to feel good. The girls need to feel good to play good." I didn't coin that phrase, but it certainly makes the point.

Wright

I've heard you say that the best coaches, leaders, etc, have a knack for seizing those subtle teaching moments that occur regularly. Will you explain what you mean by this?

Sarro

Yes, there are teaching moments in almost any situation. Youth sports mirror real-life. There will always be a cycle of both good times and tough times. Coaches are in a unique position to teach valuable life lessons. I say this because in many cases, especially during the teenage years, many players will listen to you even more than to their own parents. Be sure that your actions are consistent with your words. Show the team how to handle the good times proudly, but also with modesty. In other words, act like you've done it before. At the same time, remain consistent during the tough times. Dealing with a tough loss can be extremely difficult in the moment. But you can seize those moments to show players just how resilient and strong they really can be.

As we discussed earlier, always keep your eye on the "big picture." Very few—if any—of the athletes you coach will go on to play professional sports. However, *all* of them will grow up to become adult professionals at something. Therefore they *all* need to learn the value of practicing new skills, working within a team setting, striving toward goals, and handling adversity. If teach them how to master these real-life skills, you've given them an invaluable gift!

Wright

So what keeps you so passionate about this after all these years?

Sarro

David, it's those special coaching moments that money just can't buy. We are always searching for new and creative ways to teach, motivate, lead, and inspire. In fact, coaching requires that you literally pour your heart and soul into your team. However, there is also a huge boomerang effect. In small subtle ways, your players will inspire *you* as much as you inspire *them!* It happens during those special moments when the team or an individual suddenly breaks through a previous barrier to achieve something special. It's a natural high that money just can't buy.

It is also inspiring when you receive a letter or card from a player, thanking you for something you taught him or her or for just believing in that player. Moments like these keep me coming back!

One final thought: coaching for all of these years requires sacrifices by your family. I am blessed and forever grateful to my wife, Rosemarie, for her unwavering support for all of these years. Without ever coaching a game, she's always been my most valued and trusted advisor.

Wright

Mike, I really appreciate all this time you've spent with me this afternoon to answer these questions. I've learned a lot about coaching and I'm sure our readers will.

Sarro

Well, thank you very much for having me; it was a lot of fun.

Wright

Today we've been talking with Mike Sarro. Mike is a sports related speaker, trainer, coach, and author. His coaching style revolves around compelling Positive Expectations Methodology and his unique ability to find the subtle teaching moments that occur every day at practice.

Mike, thank you so much for being with us today on *Yes You Can!*

Sarro

David, it's a pleasure and an honor!

ABOUT THE AUTHOR

Mike Sarro has been a youth sports coach in multiple sports for more than twenty-five years. Mike strongly believes that coaches have the power to exert a positive influence in the lives of kids through the "platform" of sports. His coaching style revolves around a compelling *Positive Expectations* methodology, which he's developed through years of on-the-job experience. Another key ingredient to Mike's system is seizing the subtle "teaching moments" that occur every day.

Over the course of his coaching career, Mike has lead teams through local, state, regional, and national levels of competition. He also holds positions of leadership within a variety of sports organizations, leagues, and governing bodies. Mike is a charter member of the Positive Coaches Alliance, a Certified Instructor at the state level for several youth sports governing bodies, and belongs to the National Fastpitch Coaches Association (NFCA). He is also an active member of the National Speakers Association (NSA).

In addition to coaching, Mike is a frequent speaker at coaching clinics, banquets, and seminars. His materials are tailored to address the needs of youth sports coaches. For more information, or to book an event, please contact Mike directly at 484-431-4260 or msarro2@comcast.net.

Mike Sarro

PHOENIX Business Consulting, Inc.
228 Beacon Drive
Phoenixville, PA 19460
484-431-4260
msarro2@comcast.net

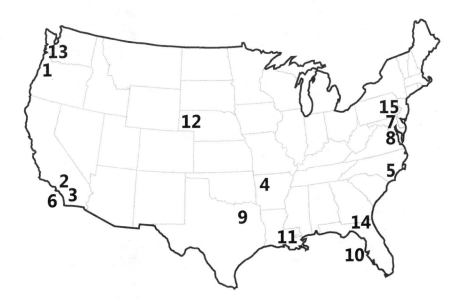

The numbers on the map above correspond to chapter numbers in this book. On the following pages, you will find page numbers and contact information for each author.

1. **Julia Marrocco**
    PO Box 5246
    Portland, Oregon 97208
    503-750-3950
    julia@mentaliron.com
    www.mentaliron.com
    Page 1

2. **Warren Bennis**
    www.WarrenBennis.com
    Page 15

3. **Natalie Cole**
    Our Weekly, LLC
    8732 S. Western Avenue
    Los Angeles, CA 90047
    323-905-1301
    ncole@ourweekly.com
    www.ourweekly.com
    www.urbanmediafoundation.org
    Page 27

4. **Kathryn Lowell**
Image Matters, Inc.
309 S. Main Street
Bentonville, AR
479-271-2134
kathryn@imagemattersgroup.com
www.imagemattersgroup.com
Page 41

5. **Howard Rasheed, PhD**
3600 S. College Road, Suite 386
Wilmington, NC 28412
877-789-8899
hrasheed@idea-act.com
www. idea-act.com
Page 59

6. **Andréa Michaels**
Extraordinary Events
818-783-6112
amichaels@extraordinaryevents.net
www.extraordinaryevents.net
Page 77

7. **Marva L. Goldsmith**
301-474-8808
marva@marvagoldsmith.com
www.marvagoldsmith.com
Page 89

8. **Amy J. Hymes, PhD**
Hymes & Associates Consulting Group
Human Resources Consulting & Training
P.O. Box 4034
Woodbridge, Virginia
703-873-7086
dramy@amyhymes.com
www.hymesandassociates.com
Page 103

9. **Jim Rohn**
www.jimrohn.com
Page 125

10. **Earl Davis, Jr.**
Create Winners, Inc.
P.O. Box 82006
Tampa, FL 33682
813-672-3445
cwincorporated@yahoo.com
www.createwinners.org
Page 141

11. **Richard Bunch, PhD, PT, CBES**
ISR Institute, Inc.
1516 River Oaks Road West
New Orleans, LA 70123
985-791-4904
Bunchisr@AOL.com
www.ISR-Institute.com
Page 157

12. **Mike R. Jay**
1132 13th Ave
Mitchell, NE 69357
877-901-Coach (2622)
coach@leadwise.com
www.mikejay.com
Page 179

13. **Lyn Jeffress**
12932 SE Kent-Kangley Road, Suite 255
Kent, WA   98030
253-239-1387
lynj@imaginedfuture.com
www.imaginedfuture.com
Page 195

14. **Dr. Monica Hardy**
Résumés & Beyond, Inc.
10646 Haverford Road, Suite #7
Jacksonville, FL 32218
904-757-5775 Phone
904-757-3770 Fax
resumesandbeyond@bellsouth.net
www.resumesandbeyondinc.com
Page 207

15. **Mike Sarro**
PHOENIX Business Consulting, Inc.
228 Beacon Drive
Phoenixville, PA 19460
484-431-4260
msarro2@comcast.net
Page 221